Outsider

The chronicles of a royal correspondent

Roger Lundgren

Editor: Paulina Bylén

Cover photo: Rickard L. Eriksson

www.royalroger.com

Translation by Aniara www.aniara.one

info@aniara.one

ISBN: 978-91-89954-64-9

Contents

Prologue

It was a calm and still summer night in Stockholm. The cold asphalt beneath my feet echoed with the solitary sound of my footsteps. I had little time to react before a fist emerged from the darkness and struck me. My head and the world went pitch black. When I woke up 12 hours later, my life had changed forever.

I'm one of Europe's leading royal correspondents, having worked closely with Europe's royal families for almost two decades. I've spent much of my adult life reporting on families sheltered by walls and bound by protocols. That night, no wall of protection appeared to me. No ceremony or title could protect me from the brutal assault and rape that left me alone, vulnerable and terrified. In the aftermath, I quickly came to terms with the fact that my life had irreversibly changed, setting me on a deeply personal journey of reflection and inner growth.

When I woke up to blood on my hands and a body wracked with pain, a wave of despair and confusion washed over me. What had happened? How had I gotten home? It wasn't just my body that was shattered; my entire world had collapsed. At first I tried to deny what had happened. I desperately searched for a logical explanation, something that would minimise the pain and fear that had now taken hold of me. But the truth crept in, step by step, until there was no escaping it. I was forced to face the darkest part of myself and there I discovered an inner strength I never knew existed.

The strength I found wasn't a powerful explosion of energy but rather a slow glow that began to burn deep within me. I'd previously been self-destructive but after the attack a new power emerged within me that I'd never felt before. Out of that brutal rape came a new realisation - a realisation of my own strength and dignity. This book is my story of how, through the most painful of experiences, I learned to stand up, fight on and eventually regain control of my life.

As a royal correspondent, I live in a world where perfection and success are often paraded. I've seen royals master their roles with a poise and strength that has inspired millions. But that night in Stockholm, as I lay there battered and alone, I felt as far from that perfect image as it'spossible to be. And it was in that abyss that I discovered something fundamental about myself - I didn't need to be perfect to have value. I just had to survive and in that survival I found meaning.

”Eljest “is a word from Norrland, my home region in northern Sweden and it means being different, special, or even deviant. To me, it carries a deeper meaning – it's about going your own way, even when society expects something else. "Eljest" expresses the courage to be yourself, to stand against norms and to embrace who you truly are. This is the foundation of the story and the reason behind the title of the book.

Sometimes it can feel like the whole world is against you. I think of all the young men and boys today who are struggling with mental illness and suicidal thoughts. I was one of them, and it's for them and their families that I've written this book. By sharing my journey, I hope to offer something more than just my story - I want to offer hope. It's not a simple manual on how to live life but it is the story of how I found my way through the darkness. And if I can do it, so can you.

How do we deal with a reality where our security has been shattered? What makes us whole again? These questions are at the heart of my life, and they're questions I know many others are asking. I've been down many times but I've always managed to get up again. That journey, with all its ups and downs, is what this book is about. It's a map of my survival and I want you, dear reader, to understand that you're not alone and that there is hope. No matter how dark it may seem, there is a way out.

My relationship with the European royal families has been both a blessing and a curse. It has given me a platform, a voice but it has also meant that I've lived with a constant struggle to maintain a facade. That night, after the attack, that facade collapsed. I realised that I could no longer hide behind my professional success. I had to confront what had happened and in that confrontation I found a new kind of freedom. A freedom to be myself without having to live up to the expectations of others.

This book is the result of that freedom. It's a cry from my heart to all those who are struggling, to all those who feel 'strange' in a world that tries to force us to fit in. I want you who hold this book in your hands to know that it's okay to be different. It's alright not to always be strong, to need help, to be vulnerable. Moments of weakness teach us who we truly are.

You are not alone on this journey to survive, to live. Wherever you are on your journey, I hope this book can be a friend along the way, a little guide.

Let's start this journey together.

The rape

It was late in the summer of 2023. I was hit on the head and knocked unconscious for half a day. The attack changed my life, how I saw myself and how I saw other people.

I didn't have time to take many steps before I saw someone coming at me at full speed. I turned around and everything went black. Twelve hours later I woke up in my own bed in my own flat. I had slept on my stomach, which was strange because I never do that. I immediately felt that something was wrong. I looked around and saw that the whole bed was covered in blood and my life was changed forever.

It all started when one of my best friends, Marianne Djudic, invited me to her apartment on Nytorg square on Södermalm in Stockholm for a birthday party on 18 August 2023. The wine flowed and was interspersed with homemade sandwich cake (a savoury dish in Sweden) and cookies. Outside the apartment, the sounds of a popular street festival in the Södermalm district of Stockholm, with artists, performances, lots of food and happy and party-goers who were thundering. As Marianne's party began to wind down, I was the last one left with her eldest son Axel. We had time to talk about life's big and small events before I decided to go home. It was 3:15 AM on Saturday morning, 19 August.

Slightly drunk, I began my seven-minute walk home. There was no sign of the party on the Nytorg square. All the people had left the square, which seemed empty and desolate. I turned onto my usual walking route on Bondegatan street, happy - both from the good red wine and from a great evening spent with so many good friends. Then the fist hit me, everything went black - and I woke up at home.

My first instinct was to find my mobile phone, bank cards and keys. Yes, everything was in its place. A taxi receipt lay on the kitchen table, detailing a journey from Södermalm Hospital to Folkungagatan street. Time: 05:15. Wow! Had I been to the hospital last night? What the hell was I doing there? In a daze I called Marianne, last night's party hostess and told her what had happened. She told me to log on to 1177 immediately to see if there was anything in my file. There I found the strange information: 'urgently admitted, left the hospital against our advice'. It got stranger and stranger. Suddenly I had two minimal recollections. One was that I was talking to a woman in a lit room and the other was that I was in a taxi on my way home. I felt that everything was becoming increasingly unpleasant. Despite a lifetime of heavy drinking, I'd never had a blackout. Never in my life. At the same time I felt something in my underwear. Oh, my god, I thought. Have I wet myself too? But it was definitely not excrement, it was a lot of blood.

I called Södermalm Hospital to ask if they had any more information about my visit during the night. But no. When I told them what I had found at home, all the blood and the pain in my body, the receptionist asked me to wait a moment. I was then transferred to the 'emergency room for rape victims'. Raped? I gasped. Of course I hadn't been raped. Because who would want to rape an ugly old queer, I heard myself say loud and clear. The kind woman at the other end wanted to arrange a visit so we could talk in peace. I agreed and also promised not to take a shower or change my clothes before my visit. Bring a clean change of clothes instead, ' advised the friendly voice on the phone. Said and done. I ordered a taxi with the address 5 Hjalmar Cederström's Street on Södermalm, at the hill before you get to Södermalm Hospital. I took the lift to the fourth floor on rather shaky legs and rang the doorbell. A lovely woman opened the door and asked me if I was Roger. She then told me that she was the one I'd spoken to on the phone an hour earlier. She showed me into a carefully decorated interview room. It wasn't the usual sterile hospital environment, which I instantly noticed as I'd been to Swedish Hospitals for mu ch of my life.

The safe environment and the kindness shown helped to calm me, despite the enormous fear and, above all, uncertainty I felt in every cell of my body. What on earth had happened to me? I swiftly came to understand that I could have fallen and hurt myself because I'm so terribly clumsy. It was certainly a possibility and a logical and bearable explanation. Soon it was time for a medical examination. The friendly nurse was joined by another nice woman who turned out to be a doctor. I was led into an examination room and the first thing I saw was the large gynaecologist's chair along one of the walls of the room. My stomach turned as I thought of all the women who had been forced into it over the years, violated and badly injured.

As a man, you don't have to sit in that chair but the examination that awaited me was still very ominous and uncomfortable. The ladies who examined me kept talking to me calmly, telling me how the examination would be carried out. What they were describing was basically an episode of the crime series 'CSI'. They were going to use a camera to document all my new injuries. And there were quite a few. As soon as we were able to locate an injury, they placed a measuring stick under it, which was then photographed.

They quickly found two large bleeding wounds on the back of my head, a strangle mark around my neck, scratches on my chest, bruises on my hands and finally a large bleeding wound on my anal opening. There's nothing particularly strange about a gay man having his bum examined. It's what most gay men get when they do their '10, 000 mile service' at the health centre to rule out or detect any STDs. But this time it was extremely stressful and the open wound they found on me stung and hurt a lot.

The medical staff then took care of my bloody underwear, which was sent directly to the police laboratory for DNA analysis. I was also swabbed for a thorough examination. After that I was finally allowed to have a shower, and it was the warmest, most comfortable and longest shower I've ever had. It felt fantastic to take that shower and, like the rest of the rape crisis centre, the bathroom was warm and cosy with beautiful tiles and green plants. Apparently there had been a patient hotel in these rooms before, which is one of the reasons why patients are spared the sterile and boring hospital environment. After the shower, I had a much-needed coffee break, consisting of a sandwich, some biscuits and a cup of tea, before receiving my first of three hepatitis injections. These are taken to give the body extra protection against various diseases.

You could say I'm used to illness. Because I take blood thinners for my irregular heart, I always have to be carefully checked if I fall or otherwise injure myself. As I had two bleeding wounds on the back of my head and difficulty breathing after being strangled in the neck, it was important that I had my head and chest x-rayed as soon as possible. Being used to spending time in the emergency room, I was well prepared for these tests to take a long time. But that evening there was a 'midnight race' around Södermalm, with major roadblocks, so very few patients had made it to Södermalm Hospital. So I got help relatively quickly. The doctors found that I had no internal bleeding, so I was able to go home after a few hours. They also told me that I had been in the emergency room the night before and that I'd sneaked home because I wanted to sleep in my own bed. This explained the two minimal memories I had of the previous day: seeing myself in a taxi on the way home and talking to someone at the hospital. As the health service has no right to force a patient to stay, I was free to go home. However stupid that decision might be. When I was finally in my bed at home, the real shock set in. It took me a while to get to sleep but before I did I decided to report this disgusting assault to the police.

In one second, life can change for all of us. In my case, I had to make a choice. Either I went down or I went on. It was live or die. It's not an easy decision and it's much harder than it sounds.

So what does it mean to choose to go on living after a violent crime? In my case it meant making a choice. I had a very strong desire to move on and one of the reasons I was able to do that was because life had not been that easy up until that incident.

I would report the crime to the police! Not primarily to catch the perpetrator but to show myself that I have an inviolable value. I also quickly mobilised my inner network, because I needed to put the event outside myself by putting it into words.

I contacted my old interlocutor, who has become a close friend over the years. She is a professional listener, trained in trauma and the best person in the world. I have a very strong sense of trust in her and she's the one I'm most open and transparent with.

I also did something as simple as buying my favourite chocolate. I treated myself to a normal, simple, everyday luxury and I think anyone who is feeling bad should think about that. We need to treat ourselves sometimes.

Of course it was also important to prepare myself for many and long periods of treatment after the trauma but in many ways life had prepared me for this event.

Growing up

I was an odd bird growing up, in a time and a world very different from today. I felt early on that I didn't belong in my home village. I experienced self-hatred and I linked my self-hatred to my sexuality. It got to the point where I tried to end my life. I was looking for a lifeline, a way to dream myself into another reality. That world became the royal house.

I was born in 1974, a year that was eventful in many ways, both at home and abroad. Sweden finally won the Eurovision Song Contest with ABBA and their entry 'Waterloo', in which the US president Richard Nixon was forced to resign after the Watergate scandal and there was a worldwide shortage of petrol due to the international oil crisis. Carl XVI Gustaf had only been King of Sweden for a year, the military junta in Greece had been forced to relinquish power and Björn Skifs was number one in the US charts with 'Hooked on a feeling' with the group Blue Swede. Sweden was a completely different country then than it is now. We weren't a member of the European Community and travelling abroad wasn't very common. On television there were only two channels and basically all Swedes watched the same programme at the same time.

I grew up in a small inland municipality in Västerbotten called Norsjö, geographically about 80 kilometres from Skellefteå and 75 kilometres from Lycksele. When I was born, my mother took a taxi to the hospital in Lycksele and I made a rather undramatic entrance a few hours after midnight on 20 November 1974. The taxi driver was terrified that my mother would give birth in the car, as she was travelling alone and my father had to stay at home to look after my older brother. But to the great joy of both my mother and the taxi driver, they arrived in Lycksele long before I did.

Norsjö, like most other small municipalities in Sweden, has big problems with depopulation, and at the moment there are less than 4, 000 people living in my home municipality. When I was growing up, the situation was very different. In my neighbourhood alone, there were children in every house and always someone to play with. My family consisted of my parents and my brother, who was four years older than me. There was also usually a long-haired dachshund in the house.

Norsjö is a village full of creativity. For more than a hundred years the people here have shown artistic talent and a great interest in sport. The first two Vasalopp (a Swedish cross country-ski race) winners, Ernst Alm and Oskar Lindberg, both came from Norsjö. So did Martin Lundström, who won two olympic gold medals in cross-country skiing in St Moritz, Switzerland, in 1948. He was a relative of mine and a very likeable person. Other sports that have been popular in Norsjö are ice hockey, football and volleyball, which is still an important sport with success nationally. Every summer there's a big beach volleyball competition and the whole community comes alive.

If you look at Norsjö's page on Wikipedia under 'famous people with links to Norsjö', you will strangely find me alongside such greats as singer Tommy Körberg, Swedish Academy member Torgny Lindgren and author Stieg Larsson, the man behind the international crime thriller 'Millennium'.

Another fun fact about Norsjö is that this is where the Keyhole Labelling of healthy food originated. In the 1980s, the so-called Norsjö project aimed to improve public health in areas such as cardiovascular disease and diabetes by getting people to eat better and exercise more. In 1985, local shops started labelling healthy products with the Keyhole label, which is now alive and well in all Scandinavian countries. I still remember how, as ten-year-olds, we would sigh loudly at some of the healthy and sometimes not so healthy dishes served in the school canteen.

At first, my childhood in Norsjö was very safe and harmonious. I had lots of friends and a loving family. My grandmother called me Glader (Happy), after one of Snow White's dwarfs, because I always had a smile on my face and life seemed relatively carefree. However, this changed when I reached puberty and my everyday life became very difficult in many ways.

I soon realised that I was different. I couldn't put my finger on what it was that made me so 'weird' but I knew that I didn't belong where I grew up. When I was ten, I discovered to my horror that I had feelings for boys, not girls. Today we have come a long way in Sweden when it comes to the situation for LGBTQ people but it wasn't always like this, especially in the mid-1980s when I was going through puberty. If you ever saw gay people on TV, it was usually clichés that were emphasised. Men who liked men were either dressed in leather or extremely feminine with feather boas. At the same time, the AIDS epidemic was raging, initially killing mostly gay men. Many people saw the disease as God's punishment and many felt that those who contracted the disease had only themselves to blame. The first gay man whose name I heard was the fashion designer and trendsetter Sighsten Herrgård, who came out with AIDS in 1987. He died two years later. In 1985, Hollywood star Rock Hudson had died of the same terrible disease and the world marvelled at how he'd managed to live all his life without anyone knowing he was gay. But the idea of him coming out as gay was completely unthinkable as it would have meant the end of his career. There were countless stars who had to hide their true lives from the world. They often lived in fake marriages with female friends or lesbians in order to be successful in their careers.

Being gay in those days meant you could get a fatal disease and it scared me to death when I realised I liked boys.

For me, the feelings I had inside meant that I could not sleep at night. Fear came into my life. It still hasn't left me and, like many people with mental health problems, I still have a lot of trouble sleeping at night. It's at night that anxiety creeps up on you the most. It's dark and quiet and then you lie there like a madman thinking about why you can't sleep. It becomes a negative spiral that doesn't go away.

I began to feel enormous self-loathing and even at a young age I linked my lack of self-esteem to my sexuality. I simply didn't deserve to exist. When I was ten, my grandfather died suddenly of a heart attack. It was the first time I was confronted with death in a tangible way. My sleep problems got worse and worse and I had to start seeing the school counsellor regularly. I had an enormous fear of death, while increasingly feeling that a person like me didn't deserve to live and shortly afterwards I tried to tie a bath towel around my neck. I still remember the feeling when it became difficult to breathe and that I got an adrenaline rush as my body went numb. My father came into my room and gave me a good scolding. Needless to say, he was scared and shaken. I managed to convince him that it had all been a mistake while I was playing - but right then and there I brought to life a demon within me that was my constant companion for many years.

I think it's important for most children and young people to feel a sense of community with their peers as they grow up. Sure - Though surrounded by friends, I was always the outcast—the 'odd one,' constantly teased at school. The environment was extremely patriarchal and all the boys had to play football in the summer, ice hockey in the winter, hunt small birds and squirrels with air rifles and take tobacco pouches. If you didn't do those things, you just didn't fit in.

I was the opposite to stereotypical inland northerners and was, as we northerners say: "nalja eljest"(a bit weird). I liked drawing, read fairytale books and loved Disney movies. Thanks to the fairytales, I could espace to different reality. It became a recurring daydream. When I was ten years old, I saw the Nobel prize broadcasted at my beloved grandmother. I noticed Queen Silvia who stepped down the grande stone stairs in the City Hall of Stockholm, dressed in a beautiful dress and with magnificent jewels. Then the fairytale came alive. That Nobel prize broadcast was one of the few points of joy that allowed me to dream away.

I became infatuated with royalty in those teenage years and have since devoured everything to do with the world's royal families. As a child, I cut out pictures from newspapers, bought books, videotaped everything that was televised with a royal connection and started corresponding with royals all over the world. My interest in royalty gave me time to breathe, allowed me to cope with everyday life and built the knowledge base I still live on today.

But being interested in royalty as a young teenager was definitely not a positive in my home country. I was bullied even more and it got worse every day. Being a disgusting queer was the most common reason for my tormentors' attacks and the days became unbearable. Wherever I went, people shouted 'femi-Roger' at me and every time it was like a piece of my heart broke. At the time I barely knew what homosexuality meant and I couldn't understand why people were so mean to me. Looking back, I can see that I wasn't an angel either and sometimes was mean to the people around me, which I understand is common with bullies. They kick those who are even lower in the hierarchy, which is both unreasonable and unacceptable but perhaps in some way it's also a survival strategy.

When I look back on my childhood, I remember one feeling that I always carried with me. It was fear. I was afraid that someone would say something mean to me. That someone would hit me, or throw a snowball at me, or that I would be 'baptised' in one of the toilets at school. When I was in year 8, I was so desperate that I sent an anonymous letter to one of the headmasters in the hope that the bullying would stop. Of course it didn't and instead I panicked when the teachers questioned all the students about the contents of the letter. Of course, I denied any involvement with the letter and I think that today's school staff and educators would probably have handled the situation better than our director of studies did all those years ago.

I also realise now that some of my worst tormentors probably grew up in a very unsafe environment. I can't even imagine what they went through at home and for me, who had such a great family environment, it was a comfort to come home every day. It was easier for me to say that the nosebleeds or scratches I sometimes came home with were because I often fell off my bike. It was very important for me to protect my parents from the reality of my everyday life and I became an expert at deceiving them. Well, it was an easy excuse to use because I did fall off my bike a lot. I was and still am an extremely clumsy person.

However, I feel like today's children have it much harder than those of us who grew up in the 1980s. Because even though school could be tough, you still had a real life after school where you could feel safe. For today's young people, the situation is different and I think it's because of social media. Many Swedish children and teenagers have accounts on Instagram, Tiktok and Snapchat and if they don't get enough 'likes' for their posts, it fuels their anxiety and depression. It reminds me of when I was a kid and the sports teachers would let two of the best athletes in the class choose who would be on each team. Of course, some people were always left out - I was one of them, I was never an elite athlete but it wasn't a big problem for me because I'm not interested in sports. But the fact that this system could go on for so many years is absolutely absurd. Anyway, my point is that kids today are never really allowed to be free. They have to collect popularity points even when they leave school for the day and I'm very grateful that I didn't have to do that.

I started upper secondary school in Skellefteå in 1990. This meant that every day I travelled by bus between Norsjö and Skellefteå, a total of 160 kilometres. The bus left Norsjö at 07. 00 every morning and we didn't get home until about 17. 30. They were long days but for me it wasn't an option to stay in Skellefteå during school. I was far too cowardly for that and I needed the security of my parents' home. One advantage was that I could do my homework on the bus, which meant I was free when I got h ome.

Although the days were long, I felt safe at my secondary school. I made new friends and had the chance to show that I was actually a good person. But one day something happened that could have been disastrous. It was the first morning after my Christmas break when I accidentally stepped into the road and was hit by a car. I was thrown several metres, hit my head and was unconscious for a long time. When I finally woke up, I was in an ambulance on the way to Skellefteå. We had just passed Boliden when I dazedly asked the nurse to turn off the radio. She responded with a smile that the radio wasn't on. The song I heard was 'En man I byrån ('A Man in the Closet)' by Lill Lindfors. Today I'm lucky enough to know Lill and I joked with her about why I heard that particular song. Was it my subconscious trying to come out of the closet? Would she help me on my way?

Many questions. Another question is why I was hit by the car in the first place. Now that I'm processing the experiences of my life, I wonder if it was also a suicide attempt.

Of course, there were many bright moments in my adolescence. I acquired a very unique and rewarding hobby early on. As well as corresponding with many of the world's royals, I also wrote to other world famous people such as politicians, actors, artists and sportsmen. I always asked for autographed photographs and very often received replies. I've had mail from Marlene Dietrich, Katherine Hepburn, Elizabeth Taylor, Gene Kelly, Frank Sinatra, Audrey Hepburn, Doris Day, Madonna and Michael Jackson. In those days, at least, those who worked and flourished in the golden years of Hollywood were real stars, and many of them saw it as an extremely important part of their job to personally respond to the huge amount of fan mail they received every day from people all over the world. Marlene Dietrich is a shining example of this. For the last 13 years of her life, she did not appear in public or meet people, spending all her time in her Paris apartment. Until her death in 1992 (she was 90 years old), she had a daily ritual of answering the many letters she received from admirers all over the wo rld, including me.

In addition, I wrote to various statesmen and received handwritten greetings from people like US presidents. I also received handwritten letters and signed photographs from Jacqueline Kennedy-Onassis, Neil Armstrong, Nelson Mandela, Mother Teresa and Princess Diana. The only autograph I immediately felt very uncomfortable with was that of former Iraqi dictator Saddam Hussein. I don't really know why I wrote to him in the first place, and I was very surprised when I received a phone call from the then Iraqi Ambassador to Sweden, asking me to get the President's photo during one of my visits to Stockholm. No sooner said than done. I visited the Iraqi embassy and at the reception, where we drank soft drinks and ate geisha chocolate, there were about ten men. All the men looked like Saddam himself, sporting his world-famous thick moustache. When the ambassador handed over the black and white portrait of Saddam in a silver frame in a red velvet box, I felt rather uncomfortable. Especially as all the diplomats wanted to have their photograph taken with the one I had received. A few years later, when Saddam Hussein was on the run and finally found in a deep pit in the desert, I sold the signed photo at an auction in the US. At the time, the evil dictator was 'hot' in the autograph world and I got more than 100, 000 crowns for the portrait. It was a welcome income at the time, as I was studying political science at Umeå university and, like most students, was relatively broke.

I actually took up collecting autographs again because one day I realised that I no longer had a hobby, as my childhood interest had become my profession. Nowadays it's much harder to get a response from celebrities in writing, as people prefer 'selfies' to autographs, which has meant that fan mail is no longer a priority. Unfortunately, those who have managed to get a response from various celebrities usually sell the pictures on ebay at exorbitant prices, making the situation even more difficult for all collectors. Many names had to be added to my collection and I managed to get personalised greetings from the likes of German Chancellor Angela Merkel, French President Emmanuel Macron and US President Joe Biden. I received a response from Donald Trump in 1990, when he was a relatively harmless American businessman who liked to be seen with various celebrities. He was happy to answer my fan mail.

After high school I was at a loss as to what to do with my life. Leaving Norsjö seemed out of the question. If I moved, I would have to confront myself and come out as gay and I wasn't interested in that. I got different jobs. I worked in a restaurant, I rode a bicycle to deliver the morning paper and I worked for several years in elderly care. It was a hard but valuable job working with old people.

I lived in Norsjö until I was just over 26. In the last few years I've worked intensively with many youth issues and that's how I first met Crown Princess Victoria. 1996 and 1997 were not easy years for Sweden and especially for the Norrland hinterland. Unemployment was rampant and many jobs were moving from the northern part of the country to other regions and municipalities in southern Sweden but also abroad to the Baltic countries. We were a few young people who wanted to focus on various social issues, so we formed a youth council. We didn't want to complain but to show constructive solutions and we had intensive contact with all the party leaders.

We visited politicians both in Stockholm and Brussels, and several of them visited the US, including Mona Sahlin, who was very interested in our cause. We garnered attention and the then prime minister, Göran Persson, wrote me a letter asking me to join the reference group of the Democracy Inquiry. We also met the president of Ireland, Mary McAleese, over a cup of tea at her residence in Dublin in 1999. She was the second female president of Catholic Ireland, the first, Mary Robinson, was in office from 1990 to 1997 and is something of a legend, having definitely broken the glass ceiling in her home country. We were also invited to the home of Britain's Prince Philip (Queen Elizabeth's husband at their castle in Scotland), which we thought was a great honour.

Our big public breakthrough came on 25 august 1997, when we hosted Crown Princess Victoria on her very first visit to a community on her own, without her parents. She was 20 years old and the media interest was enormous. She was accompanied by around 50 journalists, including German television on the ZDF channel. But everybody didn't believe in our idea! The county governor at the time, Georg Andersson, refused to recommend us. The municipality was in favour but some local representatives were astonished that we'd invited her. Why should she come to us, they asked? The royal court told us that Victoria liked the forward thinking in our letter, so she was happy to accept. I had a lot of contact with Elisabeth Tarras-Wahlberg, then head of information at the royal court, and she gave us invaluable advice on how to deal with the huge media interest. At that time, the Crown Princess was rarely seen in public as she was concentrating on her studies, so when she did appear, everyone wanted to be involved in covering he r engagements.

I will never forget the nervous morning when we welcomed the Crown Princess to the Källan Spa Hotel in Åmliden, a well known wellness resort in northern Sweden, Norsjö. In addition to Victoria, the royal entourage included a court marshal, a lady-in-waiting and Elisabeth Tarras-Wahlberg. There was also the County Governor and his wife, who thought it was great to have a royal visit. I think Victoria was as nervous as we, her hosts, were that day. She hadn't met ordinary young people her age from Norrland before and, as you can imagine, we're a bit special in a good way. The visit became a bit historic in many ways, and when we invited her to a tribute in the afternoon, with speeches and musical performances in our beautiful homestead, half the population of the municipality had turned out to welcome the Crown princess to Norrland.

We really succeeded in our goal of creating a positive media image of Norrland's advantages and our commitment. Looking back, I can say that my keen interest and knowledge of all things royal played a major role in the success of the visit. It's also a bit funny that this visit was the start of my life's journey of meeting royalty all over the world. I could never have imagined that on that August day in 1997.

For me, it was very important to find the tools in life that provided flashes of colour in a grey everyday life. The thing is, even if you don't believe it, there is always something around us to appreciate - it can be something as simple as good weather with bright sunshine. When we're feeling bad, it's easy to forget that there are positive things around us that are worth noticing. Because there are always one or more good people around all of us!

When I was growing up, I felt very lonely, even though I had lots of friends. I thought I was 'the only gay in the village', as the gay character in the british comedy series 'Little Britain' described himself but of course that wasn't true. There were several other gay people in my community. It's just that none of us dared talk about it.

I think it's important to find people who share your interests and values. Thanks to social media, you can do that now in a way that was not possible when I was young. You don't even have to live in the same country to feel connected to other people and I think that's a great thing.

Royal entrepreneurship

When I wrote a letter to Princess Lilian at the age of 12, a world opened up to me that I'd never dreamed of.

My relationship with the Swedish royal family began thanks to my contact with Princess Lilian. As you know, when I was young I wrote letters to all sorts of famous people and Princess Lilian was one of my favourite people to correspond with. Both she and Prince Bertil thought it was fun that a young man from Norrland was writing them letters of admiration and I always got funny, personal and sweet answers back. When I was 16 and visiting my cousin in Stockholm, the Prince and Princess thought I should come and see them, which I was more than happy to do. It was obviously very exciting to enter the Royal Palace and meet the lovely Prince and Princess, who took a great personal interest in me. Princess Lilian is without doubt one of the funniest people I've ever met and after our first meeting she insisted that we keep in touch. I visited her on several occasions - both at her office in the Royal Palace in Stockholm and at her home, Villa Solbacken in Djurgården. She always told me the most fascinating stories. She loved to gossip about European royalty and various relatives but she also told touching anecdotes. For example, she told me that when Prince Bertil died in January 1997, Princess Diana of the United Kingdom was one of the first to send her condolences, expressing her sorrow at Lilian's loss. Just over six months later, Princess Diana herself died in a tragic car accident in Paris. Lilian was devastated. Although the two princesses had only met once (at a party in London), the meeting had made an impression on Lilian, who was very British by nature. Of course she knew Swedish but she always preferred to speak English and since we Swedes are good at English and want to speak the language, it was never a problem for her to make herself understood. It was also standard to have a gin and tonic with her and when it was time to go home she would always laugh jokingly: 'this is the most fun I've had with my clothes on'. She had a great and wicked sense of humour.

Lilian was also on good terms with Queen Elizabeth's husband, Prince Philip, a man who was world famous for his sharp tongue. When I met him at a reception at Hollywoodhouse Castle in Edinburgh in 2000, he lit up like a sun when I told him about my friendship with the Swedish Princess. Many years earlier, Prince Philip had arranged for Lilian to get her hands on the fat English sausage bangers via diplomatic mail to the British embassy in Stockholm. This was long before membership of the European Union and in those days it was not always easy to transport food between countries. When Prince Philip represented the British royal family at Prince Bertil's funeral, he first gave Lilian a handwritten letter from Queen Elizabeth. Then he brought out a large plastic bag of sausages as a personal gift. It says a lot about their friendship and sense of humour.

Princess Lilian was a much-loved royal in Sweden and a dear 'auntie' to the entire royal family. Since the death of Princess Sibylla in 1972, neither Queen Silvia of Sweden nor the Crown Princess and her siblings had the opportunity to meet her. In many ways, Lilian had to fill the grandmotherly void, although she always joked that it was the Queen and the children who looked after her - not the other way round.

My encounters with the Princess came to an end around 2006 when she began to suffer from dementia. Her public appearances became less frequent and she spent most of her time at home in her beloved villa Solbacken with her beloved dog, the golden retriever Bingo, where they were both cared for by the Silvia sisters, who were specially trained in dementia care. When Lilian died on 10 March 2013, many people mourned the old Princess, even though she had not been seen in public for many years. More than 100, 000 people lined the cortege route in Stockholm as her coffin was taken to the royal cemetery in Haga and many Swedes took the opportunity to visit her grave and leave flowers as a final tribute. Perhaps it was the unique love story between her and Prince Bertil that touched so many. Her popularity was also due to her personality, her unique sense of humour, her great charm and elegance. Despite being the daughter of a poor Welsh miner, Lilian was truly a Princess to the core. It was a strange feeling for me to comment on her funeral on Swedish television. The Princess I had the privilege of knowing in private was gone forever.

But she longed so much for her Prince. She once told me that she and Prince Bertil always fell asleep holding hands. After Lillian passed away, I am convinced that she and the Prince held hands again. Just as she wanted.

Princess Lilian has also had a great influence on my professional role as a writer, royal expert and court reporter, although I personally am not too fond of the latter title, which is associated with gossip and invented stories. My first book, a biography of Princess Sibylla, could hardly have been written without Lilian's support. I found it very strange that there was always so much silence about the King's mother, Sibylla. After the 2004 tsunami (in which hundreds of Swedes died), the King spoke often and passionately about the longing he felt for his father, Prince Gustaf Adolf, who died in 1947 (the King was just over six months old at the time). But Sibylla was always left out of the conversation, even though, as we know, she died a long time ago, in 1972. I once raised the subject of a book with Princess Lilian, who suggested that I contact Princess Christina, which I did. Princess Christina thought it was an interesting idea and passed on my thoughts to her brother. A few weeks later I was summoned to the Royal Palace in Stockholm, where I was told by the court staff that the King and his four sisters thought it would be a good idea to write a book, so I immediately set to work on it with a view to publishing it in time for the Princess's 100th birthday in 2008.

I started by trying to find a publisher. I googled and found that Albert Bonnier's Publishing House seemed good. There was a manager there called Eva Bonnier. No sooner said than done.

I called her and she immediately took up my project, even though she'd never seen a single letter I had written. To tell the truth, I'd never written anything before, apart from my university essays but I think Eva Bonnier took a chance and thought that in the worst case, an editor would have to rewrite the whole book if it wasn't good enough. There was no need for that now, and the book sold quite well. The response from the royal family has been tremendous, and the King, his sisters and other family members have expressed great appreciation for my book. This is of course very flattering and means a lot to me. It is also a special feeling to be able to tell the life story of someone who is unable to do so, and I will therefore always have a special relationship with the late Princess, whose life in Sweden was not always easy. She was supposed to become Queen but instead she became a widow with five small children, not yet 40, and had to settle for a life of solitude, with the main responsibility of raising her only son, Carl Gustaf, who would one day become the country's monarch. The fact that there were also many rumours about the Princess because of the actions of her relatives in Germany during the nazi era did not make things any easier.

With the biography of Princess Sibylla, I'd established myself as one of the people the media always called when something "royal" happened. I also began to think about the possibility of starting a magazine about royalty. By combining interviews with history and lifestyle features, it was possible to attract the interest of many royalists and gain the trust of the royals themselves to take part in interviews. I contacted the media companies MTG and Bonnier journals and both wanted to start the magazine with me. In the end, I chose Bonnier and we started Queen magazine together, which was published in 2008. It was a very instructive time but relatively quickly my influence was more or less non-existent and eventually the owners decided to turn Queen into S magazine, which wrote 'nice' gossip about royalty, celebrities and business people. S magazine did not take off in the way the Bonniers wanted and was sadly closed in the spring of 2013. I then relaunched Queen under my own management in 2012 under a new name, 'Kungliga magasinet' (The Royal Magizine). It was sold to the media company Egmont in 2018 but unfortunately they closed it down in 2020. So I am quite finished with my newspaper career and will hardly start any new publications. The whole newspaper market has changed a lot in recent years as we consume more and more digital media and I personally think it was more fun to work with television.

SVT (The Swedish public service broadcaster) hired me as an expert when Crown Princess Victoria married Daniel Westling on 19 June 2010. My job was to explain various rituals and phenomena to the guests live on air but also to assist the commentators live on air. It was undoubtedly quite fun sitting in the TV bus shouting into the microphone 'Queen Paola of Belgium in a beige dress' and then hearing 'here comes Queen Paola of Belgium in a beige dress on the TV programme'. On subsequent royal occasions, I myself have been an expert commentator, either with John Chrispinsson (sadly no longer with us), Linda Nyberg, Ted Wigren, Ann-Britt Ryd

Pettersson, Katia Elliott, Mark Levengood, Claes Elfsberg, Yvette Hermundstad and Pernilla Månsson Colt. My task was always to identify the guests, especially the blue-blooded (parts of the nobility) ones, which wasn't too difficult as I'd met most of them in different contexts. I think it goes without saying that an expert commentator should be able to recognise these people. I find it hard to imagine that football fans would accept an expert commentator who didn't recognise every player on the pitch. Since the Crown Princess's wedding in 2010, I've had the pleasure of working with SVT on all their royal broadcasts.

Working with live broadcasts has never been a challenge - on the contrary, it has been exciting. I've received a lot of appreciation for my work but unfortunately I have also met some unpleasant people who've been very rude. The royal family stirs up emotions. Both from republicans and royalists over the years, I've encountered some strange situations and insults, even death threats. But I don't think you can take these people seriously, because they probably feel very badly about themselves. The downside of living with modern technology and social media is that some people take unimaginable liberties when 'criticising' other people. Personally, I've not been particularly affected compared to some friends and colleagues but I think it's important that people stop and think about what they've written before they press the send button on their computer or mobile phone. The only time I found it very stressful to appear in the media was in connection with the scandalous book about the King that was published in 2010. The book, which was full of rumours and anonymous sources, caused one of the biggest media frenzies in Swedish history. Because I was one of the few people who questioned the veracity of the book, I received several death threats. It was very difficult and I felt quite isolated. However, I had great support from Alice Trolle-Wachtmeister, who was the headmistress at the time and who became something of a mentor to me. She was wise and tough and had a heart of gold. Alice passed away in 2017 at the age of 91. I miss her very much.

I'm often asked which royals have made the biggest impression on me. I'm happy to say that there have been many. Queen Silvia of Sweden and Princess Lilian were the most important. But Princess Christina is perhaps the member of the royalty to whom I'm most grateful. She has a fantastic memory and judgement and has always been there for me when I had various problems and questions. She has also opened many doors for me. The fact that she herself is passionate about documenting her family history has led to many nice and long conversations between us. She has always stood up and represented Sweden but perhaps her greatest contribution was during her years as chairman of the Swedish Red Cross Committee. She also made sure that people diagnosed with HIV were supported at an early stage in the 1980s, when no one else wanted to do so. The King's sister's personal commitment played a major role in this.

Of the foreign royals I admire and have met, I must first mention the now retired Queen Margrethe II of Denmark. I have interviewed her on several occasions. The first time I met her was when I was writing my second book, which was about her mother, the Swedish-born Princess Ingrid, who became Queen of Denmark when she married King Frederik IX. I met the entire Danish royal family at their summer castle, Gråsten, near the German border, in the summer of 2009. It was a fascinating meeting and for much of my four-hour conversation with the Danish Queen I had one of her dachshunds on my lap.

I really admire Queen Margrethe. She's incredibly cool, smart, beautiful and in many ways has been a real fairytale Queen to her people. Both she and one of her sisters, Princess Benedikte, speak perfect Swedish, although it's very 30s-inspired. This is because the Swedish Queen Ingrid taught them was old-fashioned. The Queen told me that she insisted on learning Swedish as a child because her cousins of the same age (the Haga princesses) never understood what she was saying when they spent time with their grandfather, Gustaf VI Adolf, at Sofiero Castle outside Helsingborg.

I always ask the people I interview to look over what I've written, in case something has gone wrong. I did that with the Queen of Denmark, who returned my letter after a month, in which she herself wrote to me: 'Roger, this will do. I just made a few changes, M'. And indeed, she had changed the year and misspelt names. The funny thing was that she also corrected my Swedish, noting: 'write like this instead'. I had a good laugh when I saw this and thought that not everyone is lucky enough to have the Queen of Denmark as their editor.

One royal with whom I have actually developed a personal friendship is Britain's Queen Camilla. In the 1990s, Camilla Parker-Bowles was one of the most famous people in the world when the marriage of Prince Charles and Princess Diana broke up. Having always loved camilla and not being allowed to marry her in his youth (as we all saw in the Netflix hit 'The Crown'), Charles married the young lady Diana Spencer instead. As most of us know, that marriage ended in divorce and, as Charles had long had a secret relationship with Camilla, she became internationally famous against her will and for many years was one of the most hated women in the world. Camilla and Charles married in 2005 and today, after many years of hard work, she is a respected British Queen.

During the years when the whole world hated Camilla and called her a 'dragon' and a 'rottweiler', I felt a great deal of sympathy for her. So I started writing her letters and often sent her Swedish chocolate (Daim). These gestures were appreciated and I always received kind letters of thanks and an annual Christmas card. In 2017, I received a personal invitation from Camilla, then the Duchess of Cornwall, to have tea with her at her and Charles' residence, Clarence House, a stone's throw from Buckingham Palace in London.

Camilla welcomed me with open arms and we sat down in her private sitting room on the royal floor. Our conversation lasted over two hours and we discussed everything from her love of ABBA, her great admiration for Queen Silvia of Sweden's work and how her dogs were doing. The meeting was of course a lifelong memory and I know that she referred to me as her 'Swedish friend' to mutual friends. So I was justifiably very proud when I commented on Swedish television about her and King Charles' coronation in the spring of 2023.

So I've built up a large network of contacts with royals around the world. Both in the reigning royal houses and in the royal families that have lost their thrones. Until about 100 years ago, almost all European countries were monarchies with their own royal families. Two world wars and revolutions have reduced the number of monarchies in Europe to 10 but of course the old royal houses remain, even though their countries are now republics. However, they're allowed to keep their titles by birthright (a principle that has been in place since the peace of Westphalia in 1648 and is still respected). Many of these royals often turn up at the Swedish royal family's weddings and parties, simply because they are related and good friends. In the former communist countries of eastern Europe, royal families now have official status; in Romania, the royal family is recognised as a national cultural institution and receives an apanage - even though the country is a republic with a president.

In the spring of 2016, I received a call from Crown Prince Leka II of Albania asking if I would consider helping him with his wedding to the Albanian singer and actress Elia Zaharia in Tirana in October of that year. I had met the Crown Prince through our mutual friend Sadie Berisha, who's Swedish and lives in Stockholm. Together with her, I would be responsible for much of the royal wedding. My role would be to liaise with the press and be responsible for the protocol issues that are so important in these contexts.

Albania has only been a monarchy for a few years. Leka II, born in 1982, has been head of the Albanian royal family since the death of his father, King Leka I, in 2011. Albania's only governing king, Zog I, ruled his kingdom between 1928 and 1939 and was Leka II's grandfather. King Zog is perhaps best known in Sweden because his name often appears in crosswords but in his homeland he's still remembered as a great leader who built modern Albania before his kingdom was invaded by Benito Mussolini and the Italians in 1939. The country later came under the harshest regime of the eastern European communist bloc under Enver Hoxha. He isolated Albania not only from the west but also, for a time, from the other communist states, including the Soviet Union.

King Zog died in exile in 1961, leaving behind his wife, Queen Geraldine, and his son, royal heir Prince Leka, who assumed the title of King after his father's death. He married Susan Cullen-Ward of Australia in 1975. Their only child, Crown Prince Leka II, was born in 1982 in a hospital in South Africa, which at the time of his birth had been declared Albanian territory by the then South African regime.

After the fall of communism, many Albanians (Albania was the last eastern European country to gain freedom, apart from Belarus, which is still a dictatorship) began to talk about restoring the monarchy, and in 1997 a referendum was held to discuss the issue. The monarchists lost by two-thirds of the vote but the country's then president, Sali Berisha, has since said that the vote was rigged and that those in favour of restoring the monarchy actually won the vote by a large margin. Albania has remained a republic but in

2002 the royal family was able to return home. Queen Geraldine died shortly afterwards in an Albanian hospital, aged 87, and two years later Queen Susan died of lung cancer. She was only 63. King Leka I died in 2011 at the age of 72, which meant that Leka II became head of the Albanian royal family at the age of 29. By then he had met Elia Zaharia, and I met the couple when they were in Stockholm in 2012 for the 30th anniversary of Sigvard and Marianne Bernadotte's artists' foundation at the Grand Hotel with royalty from all over the world, hosted by Marianne.

Naturally, I agreed to help with the wedding and shortly afterwards we left for Albania to start planning the wedding, which was to take place in just over six months' time. Leka himself met us and we went to his stately residence in the centre of Tirana where we were given all the information we needed. The wedding ceremony and gala dinner were to be held in what is now called the Palace of the Brigades, which belongs to the president but was originally built as a royal residence for King Zog and Queen Geraldine. The wedding was to take place on 8 October 2016 and representatives of all the major religions were to be present to bless the couple.

I've really become a big fan of Albania. It's one of the most beautiful countries in Europe with an almost unexplored Mediterranean coast. It has high mountains, green valleys and is reminiscent of the places where the cartoon character Tintin used to travel. When I pointed this out to Leka II, he told me that one of the most famous Tintin albums, 'The Sceptre of King

Ottokar', has strong influences from Albania and King Zog, which fascinated Tintin's creator, the Belgian Hergé.

Albania is a wonderful country to travel in, you feel welcome and even wealthy as most things are very cheap. The only problem with Albania is the heavy political legacy it carries from decades as one of the world's harshest communist dictatorships. Many of Albania's current political leaders have links to the old regime, which is why it has sometimes been difficult to organise a royal wedding in the country. The Crown Prince is popular with the people, which of course frightens many politicians and it didn't help when Swedes came to help with the wedding plans.

I made it clear to the couple early on that the guest list was essential if we were to put them on the international celebrity map and attract the world's press to Tirana. We simply needed some A-list royals like Farah Diba (the former Empress of Iran) or Prince Albert II and Princess Charlene of Monaco. People like them always generate press, which was our goal. Now, for once, the media would report positive news from Albania.

After a week of planning, we returned to Sweden but work on the wedding was in full swing. Sadie managed to find a Swedish sponsor to print the invitations and together with the Crown Prince we drew up an invitation list that went out to reigning royal houses and royal families who had lost their kingdoms around the world. We soon suffered several setbacks. The Prince of Monaco had to decline, as he had other commitments that weekend and Empress Farah also regretted not being able to travel to Tirana. The Swedish royal family also pulled out. The royal couple were on a state visit to Germany and their three children were all parents to young children. But one day Queen Sofia of Spain (mother of the current King Felipe and wife of the scandal-ridden King Juan Carlos) said yes and then everything fell into place. Empress Farah had a change of heart and wanted to celebrate the couple as long as we could find a way for her to come to Albania from her home in Paris. The solution came from Prince Philipp and Princess Isabelle of Liechtenstein (he's the younger brother of the reigning Prince Hans Adam II and head of the family's very wealthy bank, LGT Group). They would have their private plane pick up the British Prince and Princess of Kent in London first (Prince Michael is a cousin of the late Queen Elizabeth but he's not covered by the royal pension because he's married to a catholic, odd - but that was the way it was in the UK for a long time). The plane would later fly on to Paris, where both Empress Farah and the Prince and Princess of Liechtenstein would board to travel together to Tirana. Imagine being on that flight.

Months passed and soon it was time to travel to Tirana to organise all the details on the ground in the final weeks before the wedding. From Sweden, I'd been in contact with all the media working on royal coverage in Europe and we knew there would be around 70 foreign photographers and journalists covering the wedding. We had no idea how much the Albanian press would be there. They didn't care at all about our fancy accreditation system but at least I had the opportunity to stress the importance of their registration during the several interviews I gave on Albanian tv channels. I became something of a local celebrity, nicknamed

'Mr Roger' and many people wanted to talk to me about the wedding as I walked around Tirana.

The wedding weekend began with a cocktail reception in one of Tirana's finest hotels, attended by royalty from 22 countries. One of the guests, Grand Duchess Maria Vladimirovna, head of the Russian Romanov royal family, had an urgent problem. She told me that she had flown from Madrid, where she lives in exile, and changed planes in Rome on her way to Tirana. Somewhere along the way, the airline had lost her luggage. She needed new clothes and we managed to find a seamstress to make her a new gala dress. Thank God I put my tiara in my hand luggage, the Grand Duchess said to me as we followed her to the seamstress, who created a beautiful new dress for her Imperial Highness in a flash.

The following day, the much-anticipated wedding day finally arrived. I got up at the crack of dawn and hurried to the Palace of the Brigades where the ceremony was to take place. The bride was upstairs in Queen Geraldine's bedroom getting dressed and a nervous groom was pacing around another part of the palace. Soon it was time for the guests to arrive. I had my hands full welcoming the royal guests and making sure no unauthorised guests slipped in. The King of Morocco, Mohammed VI, had sent one of his sisters, Princess Lalla Meryem, to represent him. She arrived with a large entourage of 20 people - including bodyguards, ladies-in-waiting and her own TV crew.

Other royals, such as Britain's Prince Michael of Kent and his colourful wife Marie-Christine, queued up with everyone else. I knew her because I interviewed her when I worked for Queen

Magazine. The Princess, who is quite famous in Britain for her dashing style and outspokenness, was Princess Diana's next-door neighbour at Kensington Palace in London for many years. I was surprised to learn during an interview that she had no qualms about revealing details of the British royal family's private lives.

More and more guests arrived. Empress Farah was joined by French TV personality Stephane Bern and Frederic Mitterrand, former French minister of culture and nephew of former president François Mitterrand. After the arrival of the guest of honour, Queen Sofia of Spain, and her younger sister, Princess Irene of Greece (yes, everyone really is related to everyone in the royal families), it was time for the ceremony to begin.

Both the ceremony and the afternoon reception at Leka and Elia's home went very well. What we were all looking forward to was the evening gala dinner, which was to be held in the same venue as the morning ceremony, the great hall of the Brigades' Palace. I put on my tuxedo and the robes I had been given (strangely enough, by the Georgian royal family, whom I don't know any better than anyone else) and made my way up to the palace, which sits on a hill overlooking Tirana. Once there, one of the staff came up to me and cheerfully told me that the wine for tonight's gala dinner had arrived half an hour ago. 'half an hour ago, ' I exclaimed! In my world, the wine would have been there for several days but that's not how things work in Albania.

The dress code for the dinner was a dinner jacket with cords for the men and a gala dress with jewellery for the ladies. Many of the royal ladies also chose to wear tiaras and I have to admit it was great for an old royalist like me to see all the 'bling bling' in real life. For me and Sadie, the evening was extremely intense. We had to get all the guests (about 160 of them) to their seats, greet the royals again and get the dinner started. But first we had to take group photos of the royal VIP guests and then they had to walk together to the table of honour.

Unfortunately, many Albanian journalists tried to crash the wedding party and I literally had to throw several people out of the palace. I was later assisted by the head of the Spanish Queen's bodyguard (a gorgeous Spaniard) who made sure no unauthorised guests slipped in.

As I sat down to enjoy my dinner, Sadie came up to me and told me that the original toastmaster (a relatively unknown French Prince) had fainted. He had been nervous and had had too many gin and tonics and had passed out in one of the rooms. I had to step in as toastmaster, which would have caused most people to panic but if there's one thing I know, it's royalty, their titles and how to keep them in a good mood. My grandmother was probably right when she told me when I was ten that I would be a court jester when I grew up.

The day after the wedding there was a brunch at the Prime Minister's house but I couldn't get out of bed. I was exhausted and slept for two days.

It's been several years since the wedding and a few years ago the Prince and Princess became parents to their first child, a little Princess named Geraldine - just like her great-grandmother and it will be a pleasure to follow her through life. Sadly, in January

2024, Leka and Elia announced that they were getting divorced. It was very sad to receive this news but I will always remember their fairytale wedding with great warmth and gratitude for having been part of that celebration.

I like to say that over the years I have become rich in experience but not financially. I've never been interested in covering the royal family as a journalist by indulging in gossip and I have always been open about being a royalist. Building relationships with the European royal families has taken time and losing that trust can happen very quickly. But having worked on these issues for almost 20 years, I feel confident in my position and the professional contacts I have made but as I said, there is no great financial gain in being the one who 'doesn't make it up'. My good friend Dominika Peczynski called me 'royal Roger' a long time ago, which I think is a funny and appropriate nickname and now most people call me that.

My relationship with the European royal families began thanks to my friendship with Princess Lilian and because I wrote letters to all sorts of royalty around the world.

Through my perhaps slightly different escapism, I have built a professional platform and a unique network of contacts around the world. For me, it has meant that I have been able to focus on something other than my mental illness and insecurities because, strangely, I have never felt out of place meeting royalty from around the world. They have all appreciated my knowledge and sense of humour, which has been a great blessing in every way.

Everyone has different dreams!

Maybe you want to grow flowers, start a consultancy or write a film script! Give it a go, you never know where your curiosity and interest will take you! It's better to try and fail than to always wonder what could have happened if I had dared. Trying and failing is a much greater victory than never trying. I've walked over hundreds of professional landmines over the years but I don't feel bitter about failed projects. On the contrary, I feel a deep gratitude for the many experiences I've had.

Coming out

As I entered my teenage years, I began dreaming about boys. For me, this was catastrophic, as homosexuality was considered abnormal at the time. I personally associated my orientation with self-loathing, as homosexuals were often portrayed as AIDS victims or perverts in the media and in conversations around Swedish dinner tables.

I was 28 years old when I finally accepted that I was homosexual, and I vividly remember the first time I said it aloud to another person. The conversation took place with a psychologist I was seeing in Skellefteå. Simply uttering the words was an ordeal. "I'm gay," I said.

"Oh, alright," the psychologist responded as if it were the most trivial thing in the world.

"Did you hear what I said?" I asked, bewildered.

"Yes, of course," the psychologist affirmed.

All those years of shame and lies, and the fear of my great secret becoming known to the world, and it's treated as the most natural thing in the world by him. I was astonished. In retrospect, I realise that the whole affair had taken on disproportionate dimensions, given that most people I'd encountered up to that point in my life had already understood that I was homosexual.

Yes, everyone except myself - and my parents.

A few years later, after I had moved to Stockholm and started volunteering for the Pride Festival, handling marketing matters, my mother called and asked why I was working for free for homosexuals.

"Good heavens, Mum, didn't you know I'm gay?" I replied.

"No, I had no idea," she answered, slightly shocked.

"It should have been obvious to you. I'm nearly 30 years old, have never introduced you to a girlfriend, and have been obsessed with the royal family and Eurovision Song Contest since childhood. How straight does that sound?" I wondered.

An hour later, my father called. The first thing he said was that he needed some time to digest the information I had given my mother, but that they both loved me unconditionally. However, he was afraid that I might be attacked on the 'underground' or contract AIDS, as these were the things he'd read about in the newspapers. He also thought I shouldn't call myself a 'bög' (a Swedish slang term for gay). He considered it a derogatory term and thought it would be better to say I was gay. When I explained that we homosexuals had reclaimed the word 'bög' as our own term for ourselves, he felt much more at ease. He added, "I've never met anyone who's homosexual before." Imagine his shock when I pointed out a number of people he had known for years whom he'd never suspected were homosexual.

The period leading up to my coming-out process was an incredibly long journey. Partly because I was so disgusted with myself, but also because I had been labelled as gay by my bullies early on. Therefore, it became important for me to try to live a heterosexual life. I was terribly ashamed of my situation and tried to make it work with a couple of girls I'd met through an online dating site called Lovesearch. Funnily enough, it was run by the artist and PR woman Dominika Peczynski, who would become one of my best friends a few years later.

Looking back, I think more people should go through a coming-out process. Because even though it's challenging, it's a valuable experience in learning to accept oneself for who one is. Or at least trying to like oneself.

The problem in my case was that I wasn't allowed to come out at my own pace. During my last years in Norsjö, I had developed feelings for a straight boy (something most gay men have experienced). We had a wonderful friendship, but unfortunately, we both became victims of a witch hunt by various people who felt they had the right to demand answers about whether we were together or not. Eventually, we both felt it was impossible to continue living in our hometown. The boy in question moved far away and is now happily living with a wife and children. For both of us, that time was almost a traumatic experience. I wasn't allowed to keep my feelings private; they were torn open for public scrutiny, and people I didn't even know used my soul as a doormat to wipe their dirty feet on. Eventually, I became ill. During a visit to Stockholm, I woke up in my hotel room one night with the entire room spinning. I managed to make it to the toilet to vomit, which then turned to blood. An ambulance was called, and I ended up in A&E, where they later diagnosed me with a bleeding ulcer. I believe that the pot that had been simmering for so long with my anxiety and worry about accepting who I was finally boiled over. It was a long convalescence to heal the ulcer, and even today, I still feel its effects.

For many years, my greatest desire was to feel a sense of belonging. To have friends who thought and felt like me, with whom I could talk about emotions. Unfortunately, the gay world hasn't always been the rainbow parade I longed for. There's an enormous focus on appearance in the gay world, where well-toned guys are prized and objectified. I find this very sad and cannot for the life of me understand why we've adopted the same unhealthy ideals that the rest of society has imposed on women for hundreds of years, where they've been objectified in ways that are unacceptable. Many younger gay men feel they must have perfect bodies to gain acceptance, and the ideals promoted at various parties and often in the media emphasise the perfect exterior. Given that I'd struggled with an incredibly poor self-image since puberty, it was often difficult for me as a newly out gay man to relate to the many superficial demands placed on us gay men, and I felt both lost and disappointed. The easiest way to get validation was through sex, and in hindsight, I can say that I've had far too many sexual encounters that I never really wanted. But it was a quick and easy way to gain acceptance.

As a middle-aged man, I think those of us living in the gay world would do well to examine ourselves. We definitely need a #gaymetoo movement to address how older gay men treat and objectify young gay men. Unfortunately, self-awareness is often lacking among many older homosexual men. For older straight men to publicly objectify younger women is now, usually, unacceptable. Sadly, this is not yet the case in the gay world, and I find that extremely disappointing.

For many years, I was obsessed with finding love. This is never healthy, regardless of sexuality. They say that those who chase find nothing, and in my case, it meant that I was drawn into destructive relationships that were not good for me on several occasions. I truly became codependent in other people's life situations. For me, it was a way to feel a sense of connection where I could help and support, and not just be that worthless person I often perceived myself to be. These relationships never ended well and also made me bitter. An incredibly boring and unattractive trait. Sure! I've had problems with various men over the years, but then again, that's a reality I share with millions of women around the world.

Nowadays, I'm very content in my role as a single person because even though I live alone, I'm not lonely. I have an enormous number of wonderful friends with whom I socialise, and I believe that many people, regardless of sexuality, live much lonelier lives in couple relationships than I do as a single person. The desire to belong to something larger than what it means to live single is strong for many. So is the longing for love, and many times, we humans tend to fall in love with the idea of love rather than the partner we meet or live with. Especially in Stockholm, where housing is expensive, it's always better to be two and be able to share the expenses.

In Sweden, we've come a long way in terms of values regarding sexuality and identity. But it's important to remember that the National Board of Health and Welfare didn't remove the disease classification for homosexuality until as late as 1979. I was five years old then. Sweden has been a pioneer since then, and this entails an extra responsibility not to lose focus on what's important in our world. A frightening example is Uganda, which recently introduced the death penalty for homosexual acts. We also have countries in our geographical vicinity that treat LGBTQ+ people very badly. Not least Russia, where Vladimir Putin has been driven by a strong hatred towards our group for many years. Homophobia also exists in our country, even if the situation is completely different from when I was growing up in the late 1980s. There are people who are provoked by Pride celebrations around Sweden, and we Pride participants often hear, "When will we straight people get a parade?" I think you have that every other day of the year, and if you now want a specific parade filled with love and joy, why not arrange one! Those of us who belong to the LGBTQ+ world haven't been served a Pride parade on a silver platter. We have fought for decades for the right to be ourselves, including by organising Pride celebrations. As a middle-aged gay man, I can't be anything but grateful to those who fought before my generation. It's thanks to them that we have our rights, which are easy to take for granted. For many young people today, coming out as gay is no big deal, and that makes me happy. It has even become easy to live as a homosexual in Norsjö!

Although we have come a long way in Sweden with LGBTQ+ rights, homophobia and intolerance still thrive in various places. We must never take our rights for granted because they haven't come for free. Many in previous generations have fought for the freedoms that are now a natural part of our everyday lives. This is how it should be, but with these privileges comes, as I've written, a responsibility for those who don't yet share our rights and freedoms, whether they live within or outside Sweden's borders.

The Queen and me

When I was a child, the Queen was like a fairytale creature and an escape from reality. As an adult, she has become perhaps my most important role model thanks to her uncompromising fight to give vulnerable children around the world a safe and dignified life. The Queen's commitment was one of the reasons I had the courage to report the assault to the police in the summer of 2023.

When Queen Silvia of Sweden became my idol at the age of ten, I could never have imagined that as an adult I would be able to do several interviews with her and follow her work closely. Not only in Sweden but also abroad. As I mentioned earlier, my admiration for her as a child was linked to the fact that she was a fairytale creature who gave me a much-needed escape from a grey and difficult everyday life. This admiration has changed over the years and I think it's great that Sweden has such a well-known and respected Queen thanks to her humanitarian work.

When I was 13, our teacher gave us the task of writing a letter to someone to say thank you. Most people wrote to their family or friends. I decided to write to the Queen's parents, Walther and Alice Sommerlath, to thank them for making their daughter our Queen. I found their address in a copy of the Svensk damtidning (Swedish lady-magazine), they lived at Wilckensstraße 10 in Heidelberg, Germany. A few weeks later I received a reply from the Queen's father, thanking me for the nice letter and enclosing some photographs. Many years later I was able to show the Queen the letter from her father. She was very touched because it meant a lot to her. Walther Sommerlath died in 1990 and his wife Alice died in 1997.

Therefore, it was traumatic for the Queen when, in 2011, the TV programme Kalla fakta (Cold Facts) claimed that her long-dead father had been involved with the Nazis during the Second World War. The programme, and later a book, claimed that Walther Sommerlath's acquisition of a factory in Germany was actually part of the forced takeover of Jewish businesses. For the Queen, the report caused a deep personal crisis. She did her own research, staying up all night reading, making phone calls and doing everything she could to defend her father, who was unable to defend himself. Much later, it emerged that the investigative journalists had overlooked documents showing that Sommerlath had instead worked against the Nazis, helping to smuggle resistance fighters and Jews out of Germany. Walther Sommerlath also ensured that the man who owned the toy factory had a future of freedom in Brazil. The Queen has never received an apology from the journalists who broke the story and, as with so many other royal scoops, set off a campaign that has been strange in many ways. When I spoke to the Queen about her struggle, she said that since her father could not defend himself, it was her job as his daughter to stand up for him.

In connection with this story, the well-known photographer Elisabeth Ohlson made a photomontage of the King and his friends eating a pizza from the naked body of the King's alleged mistress, Camilla Henemark. On the floor, the Queen was scrubbing off a swastika. When I saw the picture, I was enraged. Ohlson, an outspoken feminist, had degraded not one but two women in her artwork, one of whom was the Queen. To her credit, she apologised to the Queen in 2013 but I found it remarkable that Queen Silvia of Sweden had to take responsibility for her father's alleged Nazi fanaticism. As if we in Sweden believed inoriginal sin. So I decided to write a book about her. The result was 'Queen Silvia of Sweden - a Jubilee Book', published in 2013, a few months before her 70th birthday. I and the talented photographer Rickard L. Eriksson followed the Queen for a year, documenting her work, her life and her many engagements. I had the opportunity to interview the Queen on several occasions, as well as the King, their three children, relatives, friends and royal colleagues. The result was truly magnificent in the form of a beautiful coffee table book. I had also asked my good friend Maud Olofsson to help fund the project, and it was touching that so many people wanted to support my initiative. In connection with the launch of the book, we organised a seminar in Stockholm with several women leaders, where the Queen was able to talk about her leadership for the first time, and you could tell she was both amused and flattered that she and her work were being taken seriously.

Journalist Malou von Sivers moderated the hour-long discussion, during which the Queen talked about how she felt in the early 1980s when her hats were much publicised in the Swedish weekly press. She had pleaded: 'what if people could take an interest in what I have in my head instead of what I have on my head?

The Queen has long been much more than an ornament. For decades she has championed issues that were taboo for many, particularly the fight for the most vulnerable, sexually abused children, who have no voice. When I once asked her how she was coping psychologically with the great evil that all these children were being subjected to, she just said to me calmly: 'Roger, I'm not the one being raped, these children are and I have to use my voice to make sure that other children in our world don't have to suffer the same kind of atrocities.

The Queen had already founded the international organisation Mentor (1994) to combat drugs and create good living conditions for young people when she set up the World Childhood Foundation five years later. Sweden had found itself in an absurd situation where several cases of child pornography had been uncovered and brought to court. Since possession of child pornography (or, as we say today, child abuse material) for private use was legal at the time, paedophiles were able to order the evidence from the courts at a low price. Parliament did not want to change the law because many politicians felt that freedom of the press might be threatened. Children's rights organisations felt helpless and decided to appeal to the Queen. They got a meeting with her at the palace in Stockholm and showed her the horrible documents that paedophiles could order home "as a treat". Naturally, the Queen was shocked. She gave a major interview in which she pointed out the absurdity of the whole story. She added that she knew very well that as a representative of the royal family she was not allowed to talk about party politics but that she was speaking as a mother and saw the whole thing as a humanitarian issue. She immediately gained the support of the Swedish people and it wasn't long before Parliament made the important change in the law, outlawing the possession of child pornography.

At the same time, the Queen was invited to Paris by the French first lady, Bernadette Chirac, for a conference on child welfare. She had invited first ladies, queens and princesses from around the world. When it was Queen Silvia of Sweden's turn to speak, she chose to talk about her experiences in Sweden and the horror of what our most vulnerable people, children, can be exposed to. She spoke with great authority about the atrocities that exist in the form of sexual abuse and violence and there were many who felt uncomfortable with her speech. Why should this beautiful Swedish Queen speak about something so horrific that the world has done its best to ignore? But the Queen stood her ground and with the creation of Childhood, which works in Sweden, the US, Germany and Brazil, the Queen has made a real difference. She has raised up to a billion dollars to support projects that give children and young people a future.

When I wrote the book about the Queen, I quickly developed a personal commitment to Childhood. Although I don't have children of my own, I feel strongly about these issues and the important projects that childhood supports around the world. I quickly learnt that 'building orphanages' is one of the worst things an organisation can do, because so many children in institutions are sexually abused. It is much better to work on getting children into different family homes. I felt a great need to do something concrete for Childhood, so when the Queen turned 75, I raised money and personally sold the documentary 'the Queen of Children' about Childhood and Queen Silvia of Sweden's work to Anders Jensen, who was then head of Nent (now viaplay). Together with my team, I followed the Queen in Sweden and abroad. We were there when she met children, when she spoke at the UN, when she met with American donors and when she led Childhood's partnerships. We also visited Solliden on a hot summer day and interviewed the Queen with Princess Madeleine, who has inherited her mother's deep commitment to vulnerable children. I have had the privilege of visiting Solliden several times. It's a fabulously beautiful place and I know the royal family enjoys it. The mother-daughter chat went well and we had great help from the King all day, rearranging furniture, clearing away branches and other rubbish and sorting out various practical matters.

We also visited Ukraine, as Childhood has long been active in that beautiful country. We met with Childhood's partners in Kiev and towns around the Ukrainian capital. It was a trip that filled our hearts with love. This was in the summer of 2019, before Putin's despicable war of terror against Ukraine. Among other things, we met a baby who had been placed with a foster family. The baby had been found in literal trash a week before our visit. Now the baby seemed fine and the well-trained foster parents were happy to take care of the child and hoped to become adoptive parents. But today, if you google images of the street where the family lived, you can see that their house and other buildings have been heavily bombed by Russian terrorists. This knowledge is terribly painful. Sadly, I don't know what happened to the lovely family we met.

When the Queen founded Childhood, she said that it was her wish that one day she would be able to close down her organisation. Sadly, this hasn't happened and the problems for children and young people are getting worse by the day. For example, there are men in Sweden who order virtual abuse. This means using a computer to get a poor mother, for example in the Philippines, to insert objects into her own child in front of a camera. This is to satisfy perverted men. In our country and in the rest of Europe.

The Queen's whole being is filled with concern and work for the children of the world. She lives and breathes Childhood and takes every opportunity to talk about it and the world listens. Whether she has met with US presidents, the Emperor of Japan, the last three Popes or other world leaders, she has highlighted the plight of children and it has paid off. Several countries in south east Asia and one of the Queen's countries of origin (Brazil) have passed laws to protect their children after being inspired by Queen Silvia.

The Queen is definitely one of Sweden's top experts on children's rights. She has read the UN reports, knows the statistics and knows what tools to use. The now popular children's centres, which can be found in more than 30 Swedish municipalities, were established in our country thanks to the Queen, who visited an Icelandic children's centre during a state visit in the 1990s. The purpose of a children's centre is to have all the expertise, police and care in the same room and to be able to take advantage of a vulnerable child's story. It means that the child doesn't have to tell the story of their abuse over and over again, and thanks to the Queen, a large number of children's centres have now been opened in her other home country, Germany.

Princess Madeleine inherited her commitment to children from her mother, and the Queen jokingly says that her family have 'childhood for breakfast, lunch and dinner'. Madeleine is a very wise and dedicated woman. She worked hard behind the scenes for Childhood's success during its early years in the US. I once asked her what had made the biggest impression on her, and she told me about a young teenage mother in Thailand. The girl had been raped for years by her own father. When he died, her older brother followed in his father's footsteps with further abuse and eventually the girl became pregnant. Madeleine said: 'when I saw this young woman holding her baby, looking at her, she had as much love in her eyes as I have for my children.

It's easy to be passionate about these issues. But it was very brave of the Queen to take the lead at such an early stage in the fight against these taboo and grotesque acts. In doing so, the Queen has shown a new side to what her role can achieve. She clearly believes that her most important role is to support the King in every way. In the past, queens have been involved in various charitable endeavours but Queen Silvia of Sweden is undeniably unique in being the first in our time to show her courageous humanitarian commitment. If you look at younger queens today, such as Mary of Denmark, Rania of Jordan, Máxima of the Netherlands or Mathilde of Belgium, they're all working to help the most vulnerable in society. Just like the Queen. When I spoke to Queen Camilla of the UK, who works to help women who are abused by their husbands, she said: 'the Swedish Queen has really shown us all that you can and should support difficult issues. She is a role model.'

My involvement with childhood over the last few years has been with their American branch, as they have very successful fundraising dinners every year. What I've been able to contribute through my unique network of contacts are artists and interesting guests who attract media attention. It's exciting to be part of this work and I've made many new friends around the world thanks to Childhood. However, I have great visions of how we can further highlight Childhood's work in Sweden and internationally.

The Queen has many wonderful personal qualities. She has a unique ability to see people. Especially those who need to be seen, and these are qualities that her three children have inherited, especially Crown Princess Victoria. The personal support the Queen has given me over the years when my health has been failing (when I've had grief or other personal concerns) is something I will always carry in my heart. When the royal couple married in 1976, many people questioned the Swedish monarchy. The King was young and inexperienced, having succeeded his wise and elderly grandfather Gustaf VI Adolf only three years earlier. Left-wing winds were blowing across Europe and many people thought that kings and queens belonged only in history books. Not least in Sweden. But with Queen Silvia of Sweden's entry onto the royal stage, the calls for a republic disappeared, and this is largely due to her as a person. She has been a great asset to Sweden and the royal family and, as I said, I am extremely grateful to have been able to follow her work so closely for so many years.

Through the Queen's commitment, I've discovered a world that's often very cruel to the most vulnerable, the children that nobody cares about. I think it's important that we all take our eyes off our own daily lives and practice being grateful for the positive things that everyone has in their lives. It is not always easy. Although life can feel dark, it is useful and important to be able to empathise with other people's lives, because with empathy I realised that I was growing as a person and after my rape I was constantly thinking about these children. They don't have a voice but I do, and when I stand up for myself, I indirectly stand up for them.

My suicide attempts

My life has been full of contrasts. One day in December 2013, I had lunch with the royal family at Stockholm Palace. Ten days later, I woke up in a hotel room in Thailand after paramedics had pumped my stomach.

A few days before Christmas Eve 2013, I was invited to lunch at the royal palace to celebrate the Queen's 70th birthday. It was a rather exclusive and intimate event in a royal context. Invited were representatives of many of the organisations that Queen Silvia of Sweden works with and supports in various ways. In addition to some of her private friends, a large part of her family was also present: the King, the Crown Princess, Prince Daniel and Prince Carl Philip. The court staff had set up round tables in the room in Prince Bertil's apartment where the luncheon was held and I was very cleverly placed at the Queen's table with Prince Carl Philip and others.

The reason I was invited to the palace was that, as you know, I'd written a book about the Queen, in collaboration with her, for her even-numbered birthday (Queen Silvia - a Jubilee Book).

So I was very proud when I received the splendid invitation to the palace. I went with Maud Olofsson, who'd been responsible for funding the project, and when the Queen made her welcome speech, she ended it by thanking me and Maud for our work during the autumn on the book and a subsequent seminar. This gave me an indescribable feeling, given the great admiration I've had for the Queen since childhood.

Ten days after the royal lunch at the palace, life caught up with me. I was on holiday in south-east Asia and, as so often before, life felt completely dark. I didn't want to live anymore, so after a bottle of wine I swallowed about thirty pills. I remember crying myself to sleep, my body going numb, and saying aloud to my beloved father, who died in 2011, 'now, daddy, we finally meet again'.

It was my sixth suicide attempt. Looking back, I can say that I was really lucky. Despite my firm conviction that I would forever extinguish my fear and the enormous self-hatred that had long lived in my body, my life was saved. The hotel staff had found me by chance, called an ambulance and pumped my stomach on the spot. I then went back to my hotel room where I slept more or less continuously for several days. When I woke up from hibernation, I was terrified and had to take sedatives to breathe. My plane ticket could not be rebooked, so I had to make do until I got home. I'll probably never be able to go back to that place and for me that beautiful paradise became hell.

The reason I freaked out during the trip was that I'd gone there with a person I had feelings for at the time. I was convinced that these feelings were reciprocated, for various reasons, and when it turned out that they weren't, I was mentally shattered. No shade was supposed to fall on him but, as if by magic, my shame and disgust returned and so, as usual, I reacted irrationally and unintelligently. I forgot about my nice lunch at Stockholm Palace and there was only darkness and the usual self-hatred inside me. Looking back, I can see that my suicide attempts were always ill-considered and often involved alcohol. These days I only drink when I feel mentally well. In general, I feel much better when I don't drink at all, and I'm convinced that all people who suffer from panic attacks, for example, should be careful with alcohol, which can actually make their condition worse. I'm also thinking of other forms of drugs but also casual sexual contact, unnecessary shopping or gambling, as these can all lead to various forms of addiction. I've tried everything and I can say that it may help in the moment but in the long run it destroys people's lives.

How do you explain the desire to die to a person who has always valued life? Because, naturally, there's no rhyme or reason to wanting to end your life. Especially when you think of all the sick people who are dying, who want nothing more than to live on. But there's also no logic in suffering from panic attacks and self-hatred and I don't think people who've never experienced that kind of depression can understand what it feels like when anxiety takes over your whole body. Because it's not like suffering from a broken arm or a back injury. When anxiety is at its worst, none of the body's normal systems work. You can't eat or drink, you can't sleep, your heart is racing and every cell in your body is screaming and in pain. When you're at your darkest, it's hard to imagine that there's any light or any possibility of the pain going away and suicide becomes the only option for many people. That's why I think it's important that family members never blame themselves when someone close to them has committed suicide. Because when you're trapped in the tunnel of fear, there's no logic or hope for the future. You forget everything and everyone, including your family, even though you love them more than anything in the world. This has certainly been the case for me and it's a difficult shame and realisation to live with.

In addition to my mental illness, I have many other chronic illnesses. Ten years ago I was diagnosed with congestive heart failure and atrial fibrillation. A few years later I was also diagnosed with chronic rheumatism. As a result, my body is in constant pain and I have to take various painkillers and heart medication just to survive. I'm also extremely clumsy. If there is a chance of falling and breaking any part of my body, I will. As one of my medications is a blood thinner, I always have to check for internal bleeding after a fall. I've also had double sided pneumonia several times, bleeding stomach ulcers and in April 2020 I contracted a severe variant of covid-19 which took a very long time to recover from. So there have been a lot of hospital visits in the last ten years and I'm very tired of everything to do with hospitals. I can also say that these illnesses have sometimes made me feel very depressed because people around me have almost blamed me for getting sick. I don't know how many times I've heard comments like 'why are you sick all the time? A word of advice, people! Don't say that to people! It's the last thing you want to hear when you're battling poor health.

Last winter I underwent an extensive assessment to find possible diagnoses for my mental illness. Among other things, I was screened for bipolar disorder, as many people with this diagnosis are suicidal. People with bipolar disorder often alternate between periods of mania and depression and periods of relative normality. I could easily ignore the mania because I am one of the laziest people in Sweden and have never felt the enormous energy that bipolar people often get. Therefore I was not at all surprised when my psychiatrist concluded that I wasn't bipolar. If you think you have bipolar features, it's very important that you see a doctor and get a diagnosis. This is the case with all forms of mental illness and believe me, there is help available and you have the right to get help, even if it sometimes takes a long time. If you don't feel that you have the time to wait, I would recommend that you get in touch with one of the churches that offer counselling. The best counsellor I ever had was through the church and I've seen about 15 counsellors/psychologists and psychiatrists in my time. There are also many helplines you can call where dedicated people will listen and talk to those who are feeling bad and can point them in the right direction. Sometimes all you need is someone's ear. Someone to listen to you.

Now, as an adult, I realise that many of my suicide attempts over the years were spontaneous. I never planned to take my own life. I never wrote a suicide note, and I never called for attention when I acted. However, most of the time, as I said, there has been a common thread in the form of large amounts of alcohol mixed with my own panic attacks.

Let me give you some examples of what I have done while drunk that could have cost me my life. One late summer night I was balancing on the stone wall on Katarinavägen street between Slussen and Tjärhovsplan in Södermalm, near my house. There was a drop of perhaps 80 metres on one side of the wall. Why did I do it? Well, the combination of panic attacks and alcohol made me make such a stupid decision, even though I suffer from terrible vertigo.

Twelve years ago, when I was on holiday in Israel, I almost drowned and had completely forgotten about it. It was my fellow travellers who reminded me that I'd jumped into the waves at the Tel Aviv beach when it was red-flagged as a no-swim zone. I had both valium and alcohol in my system at the time and it wasn't long before I was pulled into the water. This time it was two Russians who saved my life and pulled me out of the waves.

On Valentine's Day 2014, I met an American couple staying at Hotel Malmen near my home in Södermalm. They seemed nice, good-looking and followed me home to have sex. In the gay world, sexual contact is by far the easiest thing there is but it can also be the most destructive. That's what my encounter with these guys was. Because they took the opportunity to abuse me until I lost consciousness. When I woke up, I realised that nothing had been taken. Everything was in its place. All they wanted to do was hurt and humiliate me and strangely enough I enjoyed it. Because they were confirming what I'd known for so many years. I was disgusting and deserved this kind of treatment and it was good that the suicide attempt was carried out by other people and not by me.

I also think of my friend Fabian's 30th birthday party at his family's cottage in the Stockholm archipelago nine years ago. It was a wet and fun event but I'd taken some sleeping pills when I went to bed in the morning. The result was that I didn't wake up when the rest of the house tried to wake me up, and I only came to my senses when Fabian's father, who is a doctor, sprayed me with water from a hose. He then drove me to the emergency room at Danderyd Hospital.

My last irrational behaviour happened in 2016. My friend Elias and I were visiting the gay bar 'Secret Garden' in Stockholm when I saw a dear friend, who was very drunk at the time, being harassed by a man. I went up to the man and told him to stop groping my friend. He got angry and punched me so hard I broke three ribs. As usual, my self-loathing kicked in and I realised that I deserved to be treated like this. I snuck home. Drunk and stuffing my face with painkillers. The next day I woke up in Södermalm Hospital with a drip and understanding nothing . My friend Elias, with whom I'd been out, was well aware of my mental illness and when I didn't answer my mobile phone he immediately called 112. The police had to break into my flat and thanks to Elias' quick action I survived. How can you ever thank a person for that? It's a huge thing and my gratitude toward him will stay with me forever.

Yes, there are many similar stories in my life. Each time I've survived and for that I'm eternally grateful as I embrace life today. But I know very well what it is like to have so much panic anxiety that you cannot see anything positive in life and you just want to die, so I feel a great empathy for all those who are affected by various forms of mental illness.

I think a lot about those who've not been as lucky as me. Those who may have accidentally taken too many pills, drowned in the Mediterranean or fallen down the stone wall on Katarinavägen street. That's the devastating thing about suicide. There is no buyer's remorse for irrational behaviour. What's done is done, and when you're dead, you're dead. That's why I hope that those of you who read this book and feel bad will realise that there are ways to feel good again. There are people who want to listen to you and help you with the traumas you carry. You just have to be patient and give things time. Unfortunately, I know what it's like when you're at your worst. It all feels so hopeless but I promise that you will come out the other side a much stronger person.

Dad's death

My father died suddenly one day while cutting the grass in the garden. The grief had an extra dimension because my father had been sad for months because I, his son, had been humiliated in a local New Year's Eve revue (a kind of comedy show).

As you know, my public breakthrough came thanks to being part of the Crown Princess couple's wedding broadcasts on Swedish television. Millions of Swedes had watched the broadcasts from the roof of the Stockholm Opera House and I soon noticed that some people recognised me when I was out and about in the city. There's no doubt that television has a huge impact. Many people approached me with compliments about the work, which touched me deeply. Of course, my family and friends were very proud of me but my father was probably the proudest. My father was a very special man. He was always happy and had very good social skills. I've often been told that we were very much alike, which was especially evident when we fought because we both had short fuses and could argue quite a lot. But just as quickly as the fight started - just as quickly we made up.

My parents left my childhood home in the early 2000s and moved to the village where my father grew up. They renovated an old house and had a great community with their neighbours. There is a community centre in the village where they lived, and for many years the highlight was the annual and very popular New Year's Eve revue, which attracted hundreds of people. My parents began to get involved in the association that ran the community centre. For a while my father was the house handyman and my mother helped in the kitchen. A little over six months after the royal wedding, in January 2011, the theatre group had put on a new revue, and imagine my surprise when I heard that one of the sketches was about me. My parents had been working during all the performances, so it was only at the last show that they finally got to see the revue.

Unfortunately, it didn't go as planned. The day after the show my father called me in tears. He was very upset and disappointed. When he told me about the show and the sketch about me, I could hardly believe my ears. The premise was quite funny in itself. Since I'd been involved in commentating on the wedding day of the Crown Princess and Prince Daniel, I was also supposed to comment on their wedding night. But that's where the humour ended. The man who portrayed me only alluded to my sexuality in a way that would have been unthinkable in 2011. It was homophobic, mean-spirited and embarrassing. But what upset me most was the fact that my parents were devastated by this 'parody'. They lost sleep at night, feeling betrayed by people they had known for a long time and who were actually their neighbours.

Dad wrote a letter to the local association, cancelling his engagement. Unfortunately, he never received a reply.

It was important for me to put my foot down. As you know, I was bullied in my hometown for being different for much of my childhood, and when the same pattern was repeated from a theatre stage in my adulthood, I had enough. I wrote an open letter to the local newspaper, 'Norra Västerbotten', pointing out the inappropriateness of humiliating me in such a homophobic way. I also wrote that I wasn't a unique person from outer space (which I often thought as a young person because of my situation) and that if they attacked me, they might also be indirectly attacking their own children, relatives or neighbours who might also be LGBTQ people without daring to accept it.

I assumed my article would be a big deal but I never imagined it would be as bad as it was. Just a few hours after the letter was published, 'Norra Västerbotten' had to turn off the online comment section because so many people were joining the debate. If the comments weren't homophobic, they were attacking me as a person. According to some of the commenters, I was just looking for attention and was a generally awful person. The law of Jante (the name for a perceived culture of 'anti-individualism' in Sweden) has never felt as tangible in my life as it did that day, and of course you lose faith in your fellow man when that happens. But shortly afterwards, two young people added me on facebook with the words 'thank you'. They were both teenagers from Västerbotten who had not dared to come out. It meant a lot to me, and I felt that there was a silver lining to the whole story, that I was standing up for myself and other LGBTQ people. Because if I could reach those two guys with the message that all three of us were ok, then I'd achieved what I wanted to achieve.

But unfortunately the whole incident had taken a toll on my parents. Dad found it extremely difficult to let go of what had happened and he never received an apology or explanation from the people who organised the show. On the morning of Thursday 5 May 2011, he called me during his morning walk. He was still upset about what had happened. I told him to let it go. Going over the story again and again was pointless and would only make him more unhappy. We then hung up and said we would talk over the weekend. Two days later, my mum called me in shock and told me that my dad had died. He'd died of a heart attack while working in the garden, only 65 years old.

It was a huge shock for us as a family but it was probably a good way for dad to go. Working and active to the end, just as he had always lived his life. The fact that he had a smile on his face puzzled us all until one of my aunts remarked that he was probably happy because he'd just been reunited with his mother. That insight still means a lot to me many years later.

When I flew home to Norrland on that terrible Saturday in May, I was devastated. I didn't dare sleep and wondered all the way home if I was physically close to my father when I was in the air. Because I've always believed that he and all the others you've lost over the years live on somehow. I think we humans are far too complicated as individuals and unique as people to just die and not live on.

My oldest childhood friend Anna met me at the airport in Skellefteå and drove me the 10 kilometres to my shocked mother in Norsjö. It was obvious for her to help me. If you hadn't had a ticket, I would have gone to Stockholm to pick you up, ' she said as we said goodbye.

The next few days and weeks after dad's death were like a big fog. Mum and I immediately started cleaning. Living alone in the house was not an option for my mother, and over the years my parents had accumulated things that she definitely didn't need. I don't know how many trips we made to the recycling centre to get rid of various items. Mum later found a flat in the centre of Norsjö but ended up in Umeå a year later, where my brother lived.

Losing a parent is probably one of the worst things you can experience as a human being but it's also one of the most natural, because sooner or later it happens to all of us if we don't have time to leave this earthly life before our parents. Because it's the case for all human beings, whether we are rich or poor, we are born and we d ie.

When my father died, I swiftly came to understand who was there for me around me. Grief is very hard - not only for the person who is grieving but also for the loved ones who should be supporting them. I completely understand that many people find it difficult to approach people who are grieving and don't know what to say. But in these times of social media like Facebook and Instagram, or the simple possibility of sending a text message, it doesn't have to be difficult or complicated. All you have to do is write that you are thinking of them or send them a hug.

For those of us living with grief, this gesture means more than you can imagine. Perhaps it is because we in the nordic countries are bad at talking about life and death and mourning. The catholic countries around the Mediterranean have a very different approach to mourning and they support each other across generations. I also think of the historic 'mourner' in Finnish Karelia, a woman who helped and still helps people to express their grief at funerals.

Of course, most of my friends were unconditionally there for me after my father's death and for that I'll always be eternally grateful.

I still mourn my father and not a day goes by that I do not think of him. The loss is always there but the grief changes. My father is often in my dreams and of course always in my heart. For a long time, my mother's grief was harder for me to bear than my own but I think many people feel that way after someone dies.

Dad was always so proud of me. Whatever I did, he was there with praise and support. When I had my launch party for the book about Princess Sibylla in the presence of Princess Christina, he was proud as a peacock. He was also proud as a peacock after my many TV appearances and I think that was one of the reasons why he was so hurt by that boring New Year's Eve revue. It's very sad for me to know that he died with pain in his heart because of who I am as a person and that fact will always mean sadness for me.

Princess Lilian once told me that she and Prince Bertil had a rule never to fall asleep as enemies. If there was a problem, they would solve it together. I think that's the way we should think and act in all our relationships. Because life can end at any time for any of us and no one should feel guilty about a situation that may not have mattered much.

Faith

On a royal adventure in Belgrade, I met a pigeon that changed my life. The experience was immediate and overwhelming but it would be weeks before I realised the significance of this event.

Shortly before my 40th birthday in 2014, I visited the Serbian capital, Belgrade. The purpose of the trip was to meet and interview the Serbian Crown Prince Alexander and Princess Katherine for my magazine, Kungliga magasinet (Royal Magazine). Serbia has been a republic since the break-up of Yugoslavia but it still has good relations with the former royal family. Yugoslavia was formally a monarchy until November 1945 but the country's last King, Peter II, was forced into exile in 1945. He married the Greek Princess Alexandra, and when she gave birth to the couple's son, Crown Prince Alexander, in the summer of 1945, a dilemma arose because the Yugoslav constitution required the baby to be born on Yugoslav territory.

The solution was for the then British prime minister, Winston Churchill, to declare the London hotel room where Queen Alexandra gave birth to her baby boy to be Yugoslav territory for the hours of the birth. Alexander grew up in Britain and worked for many years as a businessman. He's distantly related to the Swedish royal family and has been friends with King Carl XVI Gustaf since the 1950s. After the fall of the Berlin Wall, Alexander began to dream of moving to the land of his ancestors. He made a number of high-profile visits to Yugoslavia, always greeted by thousands of enthusiastic royalists but it was only after the break-up of Yugoslavia and in particular the fall of Milošević, that Alexander was able to plan a future in Belgrade. The privately funded royal palace, built by his grandfather and home to both Tito and Milošević during the communist years, became the permanent residence of Crown Prince Alexander, his wife Katherine and their three sons Peter, Philip and Alexander in the early 2000s.

As I'd met the Serbian Crown Prince and Princess several times before, the interview was easy. I was then shown around the palace. In the basement there was a fantastic billiards room with its own cinema. It was all very nice. Belgrade is a very exciting city and the Crown Prince gave me several tips on things to see and do and I visited several churches. In one of them I was greeted by what can best be described as a bomb blast. The floor was littered with gravel, a few windows were shattered but what struck me most was that a mural of Jesus had been destroyed. Someone had gouged out the eyes of the painting and it looked terrible. I asked my guide what had happened and he told me that the church had been destroyed by the communists during the many years of dictatorship. The communists never appreciated the Christian faith, so the current regime wanted to preserve the desecration of the church building because it was also part of our history.

It was a very special experience for me. Since my father's death, my grief had been very real and many thoughts about life and death had come to my mind. I had a basic Christian faith and was confirmed but I had hardly ever read the Bible. But it was terrible to see the battered figure of Jesus. So I leaned against the wall and thought about it. Suddenly there was a flutter at my feet. I looked down and saw a bird flying towards me. It circled around me and it felt as if we'd made contact. I know it sounds crazy. But for a moment my whole body was filled with love and without exaggeration it was the most euphoric feeling I have ever experienced. I was completely numb and felt like I was going to pass out. I had to get back to the hotel. When I got there, I collapsed in my bed. I don't know how many hours I slept but it felt like I 'd run a marathon. That's how physically and mentally exhausted I was.

I found it quite difficult to let go of my experiences in Belgrade, even though I couldn't put my finger on what had happened. Some time after my return to Stockholm, I called my friend Viveca Bratt, who had been the friend I mainly spoke with for a number of years. I met Viveca through mutual friends Carola Häggkvist and photographer Rickard L. Eriksson, and at the time she was working at Klara Church (opposite Åhléns city in Stockholm). Klara Church is one of the Christian churches in Sweden that does the most tangible good for those who need it most. They work hard for the homeless with soup kitchens, use the church as a dormitory, help poor families and support prostitutes in a modern and committed way. Viveca is without doubt one of the wisest people I've ever met, as is her husband Hasse, who's a priest. She became my counsellor and we had many deep conversations together. Thanks to her I was able to identify old bagage that I'd been carrying around with me all these years. When I returned to Sweden after my visit to Belgrade, I went to see Viveca in the Klara Church and told her about my strange experiences in Serbia. She listened with interest and asked, 'what was that bird that flew towards you? ' to which I replied that it was a white dove.

Fascinated, she took me into the church and pointed to the ceiling above the altar and asked me what I saw there. Yes, a dove, I replied. There was also a dove above the pulpit, as is the case in many Swedish churches. I had to admit that although I'd always thought of myself as fairly well educated, my knowledge of the Bible was perhaps not the best, but of course I knew about the trinity of God, Jesus and the Holy Spirit. What I didn't know was that when God takes on a human form, it's often in the form of a white dove. You could describe it as the Holy Spirit making himself known and the people who experience such an encounter are extremely privileged. It's through the Holy Spirit that God can live among us on earth, bringing life, comfort and love. The pieces of the jigsaw fell into place. I'd looked countless times over the years for signs of God's existence and a sign that my father was well and it happened in Belgrade, of all places, during one of my royal adventures. That I should encounter my Christian faith in a chaotic castle chapel in one of the Balkan countries was completely unexpected and what I felt was my father's presence. I know it' s difficult to explain and may seem strange to people who haven't experienced it.

When I had time to digest my experience a few weeks later, I felt guilty. Here I was, living like a bandit, partying and barely leafing through a Bible, gliding by without difficulty in front of many literal believers who had never experienced the greatness I had. And one thing is for sure. Since experiencing and learning about this event, my life has been changed in many ways. I don't doubt for a second that God exists and that there's life after death. I know that my father and others I've lost over the years are well. Calling yourself saved sounds really pretentious, especially when you, like me, still live like a donkey sometimes and are not particularly pious. But I'm working on it.

For many people, belief in God is controversial. I have a lot of friends who think I'm super provocative when I tell them I'm a believer. That's completely incomprehensible to me. Our whole society is based on Christian values, we are born, we are baptised, we are confirmed, we go to Christmas mass, we get married and finally we are buried. Most Swedes, 5. 8 million, belong to the Church of Sweden and attend one of our 3, 400 churches around the country.

One person who was deeply religious was my beloved grandmother Bertha. She was born in 1908 and left this earthly life in 1995, a year in which I was unfortunately living abroad. To this day I regret not being able to attend her funeral, as I feel it's an important part of the grieving process. We were best friends. Gran was a very special lady who was loved by all. Her door was always open and she made waffles every day. Waffles that, decades later, I can still fully appreciate the smell and taste of.

She loved the royal family and we had many amusing conversations over the years. As I said, Christianity was important to my grandmother and she often talked about her view of God. I was 16 at the time and completely uninterested in anything to do with religion. When my grandmother died, she left me her Bible, which had been read to pieces and even taped together. The bible was left in a cupboard and it was only after my father's death that my mother and I found my grandmother's old Bible. I didn't think much of it at the time and put the Bible in my mother's cupboard. In the summer of 2023, when I was cleaning out my mother's apartment, I found my grandmother's torn Bible. I began to leaf through it, and in several places she had left handwritten messages for me. It gave me chills to read her little pieces of advice and encouragement. It was as if she could see into the future and was communicating with me from the other side, so many years after her death.

A few months later I was on a plane to New York with my dear cousin Carola. I told her about my grandmother's Bible and she was also touched by what I said. When we arrived in New York, we met up with my friend Viveca bratt from Klara Church to attend Childhood's big fundraising dinner together. And as we walked around, who did we meet? Well, the Serbian Crown Prince and Princess, who were visiting New York and wanted to see the Queen, and Princess Madeleine. It was with them that I had my first encounter with my faith and the white dove, and since Viveca was the one who explained the whole situation to me, it felt like I had come full circle.

For me, faith is very simple. I believe that I and all my fellow human beings are far too advanced as individuals to be descended from apes. And when something terrible happens, when someone close to you falls ill or your life is threatened, what do many non-believers do? Well, they say a prayer. We also think of ourselves as very rational people but are we really? For what can make us feel better than anything else, or worse than we can ever imagine? Yes, love! And it doesn't have to be rational whatsoever. Who among us hasn't fallen in love with the wrong person, even though we knew all along that they weren't right for us?

It's also interesting that in moments of local and national crisis - such as a tragic death affecting an entire village, a fire in a Gothenburg discotheque, the assassination of a foreign minister or a terrorist attack on Drottninggatan street - where do people turn for comfort? To the churches.

The Church is an important social actor when it comes to mental illness. They work both in prevention and in care and they know how to listen and empathise.

The Church has many roles to play in supporting people who feel unwell. If you look at the Church of Sweden's website, you will see that, for example, they comfort deaf people who are feeling unwell via videophones, you can contact an on-call priest, where everything you say is confidential, or you can get counselling from one of the Church's deacons. Churches also help people who are grieving, they have great expertise in talking to victims of sexual abuse, they can provide family counselling and they also work in hospitals, prisons, universities and the armed forces.

As someone who is alive because of the help I received from the Church, I cannot stress enough how important it is to try to contact one of their many staff. They really have a lot of experience and they help many Swedes who feel bad every day. Something to think about for all those who are stuck in the long queues for psychologists and vital help.

I think it's important that we as people try to get in touch with our spiritual sides. I'm not saying run to the nearest church and become a believer. It's not about religion or faith, it's about affirming your inner self. It's like there's something in there, call it the spark of life, that's indestructible. Sometimes we feel it clearly and sometimes it feels like it has left us. For me, faith was the path to my spiritual awakening and thus contact with the spark of life. For others it may be yoga, meditation, astrology or experiences in nature. I cannot stress enough how important it is for us humans to get in touch with our inner selves. We are so much more than a physical mass walking the earth. It's important to think holistically, from a holistic perspective. Because if we don't feed our souls, our inner selves, the spark of life, then our bodies won't work.

A conversation with the Crown princess

In 1997, I invited Crown Princess Victoria to visit my home municipality of Norsjö to draw media attention to sky-high youth unemployment. Victoria accepted. 30 years later, we met in the same place and it became one of the most important conversations of my life.

One day in the summer of 2017, I was approached by the Head of Business in my home municipality. He was delighted to tell me that Crown Princess Victoria would be visiting Norsjö in September as part of her regional tour of Västerbotten. The municipality wondered if I would consider coming home and playing host on the day when the Crown Princess would, among other things, inaugurate a newly built outdoor sports facility.

As it was exactly 20 years ago that I first met Victoria in Norsjö, where I'd invited her as chairman of the local youth council, it seemed very appropriate to welcome her back. In connection with the Crown Princess's 40th birthday on 14 July 2017, she expressed a wish to the country's county councils to visit all 25 Landscapes (a non-political division of Sweden based culture). She wanted to meet local representatives of companies and organisations and to show the world Sweden's beautiful nature, thanks to the many journalists and photographers who always accompany her on official trips. The hikes took almost two years to complete, and Västerbotten, where I come from, was the Crown Princess's second visit to the region.

Returning to my home county has always been stressful because of the many difficult experiences I've had there. The day I was to host the royal inauguration was a really grey October day. My mother and I drove the 16 kilometres between Norsjö and Umeå, where my mother had lived for a few years. When we got there, I could see that the new sports park that the municipality had built on the old gravel field where I had had hundreds of hours of football, athletics and beach ball had become quite beautiful.

I just had time to prepare my instructions for the day when the Crown Princess and her entourage arrived. As I greeted Victoria, she laughed and said: 'Now we're back on track, Roger'.

And indeed, she was right. Two decades after our first meeting, we were back in Norsjö but this time I was not at all nervous about meeting her, as I knew her well, having met her many times before. Over the years I have seen at close quarters how incredibly good the Crown Princess is at talking to all kinds of people. Not least children, which was very evident during the visit to Norsjö and I don't know how many selfies she took with the youngest members of the audience. Together with the children, Victoria also tried out all the activities in the sports park. She even took the time to comfort a little boy who was crying and asked why she wasn't wearing a crown. It's a question I've heard many times from royals across Europe and victoria knew exactly how to handle the situation. She put her arm around the boy and told him that she only wore the crown at really nice parties and not in everyday life when she went out to play sports.

Crown princess victoria and I also had time to take a little walk and talk about this and that when she asked me how it felt to be back home. I realised that although my roots are in Norsjö, it's not home anymore. I'd lived in Stockholm since 2004, and my mother had moved to Umeå when she became a widow, because we lost my father in 2011.

I also told her that it felt very strange to walk around with her in my old schoolyard, where I had felt very bad for many years and that one of the most important things to get through those years was my interest in her family and especially her mother.

A fact that touched her very, very deeply.

When we said goodbye later that day, she said, 'See you in Stockholm and say hello to your mum'.

I told her that my mother was standing next to me and the Crown Princess shook both of her hands and said:

'What a competent son you have'.

Neither my mother nor I could believe our ears and we were very excited when we drove back to Umeå.

That day became a great memory and was especially important to me in 2019 when my mum had a massive stroke. She was unconscious for several days and when she woke up, I moved in with her for almost four months to help and support her. I was grateful that I'd worked in the care sector when I was young and had learnt how to look after other people. Mum has had a pretty tough time since her stroke, especially during the pandemic when she, like so many others, had to spend most of her time alone. She had a lot of trouble with one of her legs and would fall. Over and over again. My older brother and I had to fight the Umeå municipality for several years before she finally got a place in a nursing home. She'd fallen several times and hurt herself very badly. Now she lives in a nice place and gets good care, However it's very sad that it's so difficult for our elderly to get the help they are all entitled to. If you don't have someone to fight for your rights, you can easily end up outside the welfare system, despite all the tax money you've paid over the years. Unfortunately, there's usually no interest in our oldest residents during elections, by most political parties. Perhaps they don't generate enough votes. In any case, it's terrible.

Two years before my mother's stroke, we lost my cousin Linda. She was a year older than me and we had grown up together. She was only 44 when she died of an aggressive and merciless cancer. Linda left behind a family with a husband and two young children. Her death left a huge wound in my heart and since her death I have felt a responsibility for life. For my own life but also to live for her and that's a great responsibility. I'd always seen her as my natural link to Norsjö, because she never left our home parish. When we were old, we remembered old times and relatives we both loved.

We talked about grandma's good waffles and funny pranks. Now that's over and it's terribly sad.

Linda's death and later my mother's stroke were two huge personal crises that turned my life upside down. But an important reason why I was able to cope with these situations was actually the kind words I heard from the Crown Princess when she visited my mother. It was then that I felt the circle of my life closing. At home, I had one of the most beautiful conversations I'd had in years with a member of the royal family and this realisation, along with my newfound faith, made me decide to give up what had been an almost lifelong battle against myself with fear, hatred and destructiveness. I was finally ready to start liking myself. I'll also be forever grateful to the Crown Princess for giving me and my mother such a beautiful memory to share.

In terms of work, I had finished my documentary for viaplay with the Queen, and Princess Madeleine when the terrible pandemic hit in 2020. Like everyone else working in the media, it was two lost years. Both financially and personally. After the pandemic, we sold the documentary 'the King's Inner Circle' to Viaplay, with me as executive producer. It would be about the King and his life and would be released in 2023 to coincide with his 50th year on the throne. Usually royal anniversaries are not well covered but this time, to our great surprise, all the media houses were on board. SVT had two documentaries, TV4 had one, we had ours on Viaplay and Kanal (channel) 5/Discovery had a series that was also shown on HBO. I was shocked, to say the least, by the level of interest and realised, together with my talented team, that we needed to find a special approach to the series that would make our programme unique. So we decided to focus on the King's entourage - his wife the Queen, his sister Princess Christina, his cousin Queen Margrethe and his childhood friends (who'd never spoken to journalists before) were asked to tell his life story instead. The result was very good and attracted an audience of millions.

Of our competitors, I was most impressed by TV4, whose series 'The Throne' produced a great documentary in which the King himself, in good humour, shared his many memories of his years as Head of State. One of SVT's documentaries, 'The King and I', by filmmaker Karin af Klintberg, received a great deal of media attention. I felt very ambivalent about it. It was warm in many ways and gave a good picture of the monarch but it was also somewhat uninhibited with personal questions, showing an uncomfortable King and a journalist who wanted to be in the picture as much as the King himself. When I have filmed with royalty, I've never been in front of the camera. Many times I've even made sure that my voice was cut out. I'm of no interest in this context. It's the royals who tell the story that the audience wants to see and hear. Not us journalists.

In connection with the production about the King, I was asked by people close to the King if I would consider writing a biography about him. I immediately rejected the idea. Writing a book is hard work and, having written three royal biographies, I felt done. But the more I thought about it, the more I realised that the King deserved a biography that took him and his role seriously. Very few books have been written about King Carl XVI Gustaf over the years. They've mostly been various commemorative books produced on even-numbered birthdays, and the only real biography written about him was the scandalous 2010 book ’The Reluctant Monarch', which was largely a patchwork of old rubbish, anonymous sources, insults and a lot of lies. Despite the book's, to put it mildly, poor sources, it had a huge impact, not only in Sweden but also abroad, because it claimed that the King had socialised in criminal circles and had cheated on the Queen. The book could have had enormous consequences for the Swedish system of government, which I think was the purpose of its content.

So I decided to write a book. After all, I'd accumulated knowledge during much of my life and had been able to document my meetings with people like Prince Bertil, Count Sigvard Bernadotte, the British Prince Philip and other relatives and associates of the King who are no longer alive. Unlike other journalists, I also had many conversations with the King himself, his entire family and royalty throughout Europe. As I pointed out in an earlier chapter, this trust has taken a long time to build and has not been given to me for free. Public figures in general and perhaps royalty in particular, are often cautious, afraid of being betrayed and having their trust broken. I often say that I am in the business of trust and that trust can be lost very quickly if you make the wrong move.

While I was producing television, conducting interviews, putting out fires and doing research for my series, I was also writing my book. Of course, I couldn't have done it without my colleagues and a fantastic team. During this time, I suffered health problems again and had to spend a week in intensive care at Danderyd Hospital. The idea was that during this time I would accompany the royal couple on a state visit to Jordan. That was out of the question. I was pretty much under the radar in Hospital but I managed to write two chapters at least and when I recovered in the spring of 2023, it was full steam ahead with both the book and the TV series.

I was very happy with both products and was well prepared for the 29th of August, when both the series and the book were launched in large parts of the Swedish press. What I couldn't imagine at the time was that my life would once again be turned upside down and this time I would need all the strength I could ever muster.

The meeting between my mother and the Crown Princess in my old schoolyard was a wake-up call for me. I realised that I deserved to feel good and be proud of myself. Because when the Crown Princess took my mother's hand and said that her son was good and someone to be proud of, she was affirming me through my mother. All people need to be seen and affirmed, in my case it happened to be a Princess who gave me recognition but affirmation is equally valuable wherever it comes from.

The aftermath

After the rape, a machine went into action in the form of police interviews, trauma counselling, insurance claims and conversations with loved ones. With my whole life 'on fire', I had to deal with all the practicalities, large and small, that come with being a victim of crime. A world I had no idea existed.

As my life had been generally up and down for a long time, I was in a way prepared for the assault and rape I suffered on 19 August 2023. When I woke up after my incredibly difficult ordeal, it was Sunday afternoon. Which was good because I needed to sleep in, be alone and collect my thoughts before going to the police. I'd decided to go to the police station on Kungsholmen on Monday morning to make a report.

Before I went to the police, I saw the jumper I was wearing when I was attacked lying in a corner of my bedroom. It was a pink jumper with the words 'yes homo' on it. I had bought it to wear at the opening of pride in Stockholm this summer. Maybe it was relevant to the police and the investigation! What if I had been the victim of a hate crime? The jumper, like my other clothes, was stained with my own blood. When I arrived at the police station,

I took a note of the queue and waited my turn. It was undeniably very uncomfortable to sit in a public room and talk about what I'd been through over the weekend. The policewoman wrote down all the details and assured me that I would be contacted by her colleagues soon.

The next few days were a blur. Among other things, I had several meetings with Södermalm Hospital. They gave me a few weeks' sick leave. That's as long as you can be on sick leave in Sweden after being raped. After that, you are expected to be able to work again - even though you have been through an indescribable experience. In addition to meetings with the health services and the police, it was also important to explain to my insurance company what I'd been through. All of this was very stressful. Especially as my life had been turned upside down. I was also physically fragile after all the injuries and for several days I found it very difficult to speak because the perpetrator had tried to strangle me.

During this process I had several meetings with the police. After I made my first report to the police, I was assigned a lawyer who attended all the interviews, acted as a bridge between me as a victim and the police, and represented me at the district court if there was a trial. I was treated fantastically well by all the agencies and people I met. I was seen and everyone listened to my stories and yes, the police thought it was significant that I was wearing the jumper that I was wearing. That it might have triggered unacceptable feelings in another person that led to the assault.

The weeks after the attack felt macabre in many ways. I did a lot of interviews, both for my new book and for the TV series about the King. When I look back at my appearances on

Go'kväll' and 'Nyhetsmorgon', I can clearly see my stunned expression.

How the hell do you manage these interviews? ' one of my friends asked.

You know what you're supposed to do. ' I replied a little cockily but now that I've gained some distance from that time, I realise that it all became a lifeline for me. It was incredibly nice to be able to talk about King Carl XVI Gustaf and his life and not have to deal with my own shit all the time. That's what I was doing anyway with the medical staff, the police and my friends. As SVT's broadcasts on the King's 50th birthday were approaching, I decided to tell my colleagues what I'd been through. This was in case I felt it would be too stressful during the long live broadcasts that would last for two days. But I didn't have to worry. Everything went smoothly and, once again, my passion for royal history became a life line to hold on to when the rest of life was a stormy sea doing its best to drown me.

However, I had to cancel my planned book launch. I had booked the Baroque Hall at the History Museum and a panel consisting of former Centre Party leader Annie Lööf, author Johan Hakelius, former court information officer Elisabeth Tarras-Wahlberg and columnist Susanna Popova, where we were to talk about the King's life in front of 300 guests. Unfortunately, I found it impossible to organise the event with so many people. I was very tired.

In one of the interviews I was asked if it was possible that the attacker had seen that it was me he was attacking. No, ' I replied immediately, 'my fan base is made up of older ladies who like the royal family. They don't go out at night to knock on gay doors.

There was no doubt in my mind that the person who'd done me all this damage was a man. Firstly, only men behave that badly, and secondly, my last memory before I lost consciousness was of a man lunging at me. Unfortunately I couldn't give a better description. I was ashamed, and it was a recurring feeling for a long time. Shame. Shame for getting too drunk that night. Shame for not going home earlier from the party. Shame for wearing that pink shirt with 'homo' on it.

I also felt tremendous shame that, as a man, I was trespassing on the territory of raped women in the gender-neutral clinic where I was being treated. As both women and men are treated in the same ward, I ended up there and later received my trauma treatment. However, I was worried that some of the vulnerable women would feel uncomfortable with my presence in 'their ward' as they all ended up there because of men. Although all the staff stressed that I had as much right to be there as the female victims, I found it incredibly difficult. Which made me feel even more ashamed. I was also ashamed of using police resources. At a time when Sweden has become a 'Wild West' with daily bombings and children murdering other children, I didn't want to take up their valuable time.

The rape crisis centre assigned me a trauma expert called Anna, and my conversations with her were extremely valuable. She immediately asked me how important it was for me to write down the whole course of events. For many victims it's very important to know every minute of the assault, while others do not want to know at all. For them, the uncertainty is what keeps them going. I could not say what I felt. But it was extremely uncomfortable to learn in a new interview with the police that they'd not been able to see me on any CCTV near the scene of the crime and that I'd not been taken by ambulance to hospital immediately after the assault, as I had intended. The police had also contacted all the taxi companies to find out if any of them had taken me to a&e. But no. None of them had taken me. We also went through all my apps and bank statements and there was no trace of how I'd gotten to the hospital. So there were two theories. Either I'd walked from Nytorget square to Södermalm Hospital. That's usually a walk of about half an hour - or more if you have rheumatism like me. The other possibility was that someone had driven me there. Maybe it was even the perpetrator who felt guilty and left me there. I asked the police if they couldn't see on the CCTV outside the hospital entrance how I got there but I was told no, there was no camera there. How is that possible? In these times of high levels of crime? You don't have to be a Nobel prize winner to realise that both victims and perpetrators pass through that entrance several times a day, and that a camera would also protect all those who work in emergency care. We Swedes are naive, and I am aware that there's an intense debate in our country about the usefulness of surveillance cameras. Critics of these cameras argue that they don't want to live in a surveillance society and that their privacy should not be violated. As a victim of crime, I think like this: if you're not hiding anything, you won't be offended by being filmed, and if that's how we can have a more law-abiding and safer society, then the state can put cameras in every neighbourhood. Because no one should have to go through what I went through in the autumn of 2 023.

When I left the police station near Mariatorget square after my new interrogation, I had a lot to think about. I was confident that someone had called 112 (emergency number) and that I would get the help I needed. I immediately ruled out going to the hospital myself. How could I walk for an hour if I was unconscious? It must be physically impossible. At least in my case. And if I hadn't gone myself, who would have taken me? As usual, I turned to my old counsellor, Viveca, who listened and said: 'it could actually be an angel who helped you. I don't mean an angel with wings on his back but a fellow human being who wanted to be there for you. This theory gave me great comfort and strength, and it's the explanation I chose for how I got to the hospital, even though I left an hour after I got there.

I believe that we humans are forced to face the kind of criminal case I was exposed to. It's not possible to ignore such a turbulent event. At first I felt my life was ruined. Now I think it's changed. Because for me there is a before and after date with this traumatic event. I felt and still feel that I have two choices. Either I let this experience destroy me. Or I don't. It was not difficult for me to choose option two. Maybe it's because of all the other hard things I've been through in my life, and today I feel like a very strong person. But there are some things I've had to change and work hard on. For example, I don't want to listen to music when I go for my daily walks. It's important to me that all my senses are 100 per cent present when I'm walking among people. I also found it difficult to be in public places and preferred the safety of home. When I got off the bus, I was happy to stand beside it and let people pass. The feeling of someone walking behind me is still annoying and I've realised that the only way to get over it is to expose myself to these situations again and again. So that you learn to feel safe. My psychiatrist told me that it is important to master the situations where you feel unsafe, like when you are in the city, surrounded by all the people. Stop, let them pass by. Nothing will happen. It was a useful exercise. It's an effective way of working with all kinds of phobias. If you are afraid of birds or dogs, you have to learn to approach them because they're everywhere. If you are afraid of snakes or tarantula spiders and you live in the centre of Stockholm, you may not need to focus so much on this because these animals do not affect your daily life. But we're all surrounded by people. At least if you live in the capital city.

There are many things I have thought about after this experience. The senseless violence that is constantly increasing. The fact that we sometimes dehumanise the human in all human tragedies, forgetting that every number in the statistics is one of our fellow human beings. I also thought about the high level of stigma that many male victims of crime feel. Perhaps it was easier for me, as a homosexual, to report the crime I was subjected to than for a heterosexual man. For me, the masculine image is not something I think about. I am who I am. We men rarely think about the fact that we might be attacked. That's not the case for women. When I started talking to my female friends about these issues, most of them told me that they often went home with their keys in their fist between their fingers as a weapon, in case someone attacked them.

I also thought a lot about the three women who were raped in the two weeks before I was raped in Södermalm. In the same area. Maybe there was a connection and I have a lot of sympathy for what they went through.

Because I told several people what I'd been through, the information about the incident spread like wildfire in all directions. Therefore it was important for me to be able to tell the story in my own words to people who are close to me in different ways. The most difficult conversation was with my mother. The first thing she said when she found out what had happened was: 'this is what my dad and I were afraid of'. She was referring to the conversation I had with my parents in 2002 when I told them I was gay and my father said that although they loved me unconditionally, they were afraid I would get AIDS or be abused by homophobes. Mum's reaction was expected but it still hurt. You're always a parent to your children. My closest friends have been incredibly concerned and supportive and have done their utmost to make me feel safe. As I have good private health insurance with Folksam (a Swedish insurance agency), in addition to the usual support from the company, I've also had the opportunity to meet privately with a psychiatrist and have about ten sessions of psychotherapy, where I've learned various relaxation exercises and how to work with my body when I feel stressed.

In October 2023, as mentioned earlier, I travelled to New York with my cousin Carola to attend a fundraising dinner for Childhood. As I have a charitable commitment to the organisation and had managed to arrange the entertainment with my good friend Viveca Bratt in the form of british artist Natasha Bedingfield, it felt important and right to be there. The dinner was a great success and we managed to raise more than 10 million crowns for Childhood's important work. For me, it was an important break to be able to travel. I've always been close to my cousin and it was wonderful to go away with her. I'd emailed Princess Madeleine before the trip to tell her what had happened to me and, like everyone else, she was shocked. I'll always be grateful for the wonderful support she gave me during this time. The Queen usually attends the American fundraising dinners and usually insists on visiting the UN Building and attending seminars on children's rights. So it was on this occasion. When she spoke about the suffering of so many children in our world at this time, both in Ukraine and in the Middle East, it put things into perspective. Who was I to complain about my situation when I am a privileged middle-aged Swedish man, despite what I've been thr ough!

But at the end of November a new blow came. The first snow had fallen like a white blanket over Stockholm and as I was walking to the bus I suddenly lost my footing. I went up in the air like a cartoon character slipping on a banana peel and landed like a pancake on my left hip. The pain was immense and I screamed. I immediately realised that I'd hurt myself badly as I lay on the ground at the bus stop. Although there were about ten people there, no one asked me how I was feeling. I don't know how I got up but the first thing I decided to do was ignore the incident. Having been to a&e ten times in the last three years, I wasn't interested in going there again. But after three days I had to change my strategy. I'd developed a high fever and was having difficulty moving. I went to Cityakuten (an emergency centre) on Hötorget square and after many hours of waiting, a doctor said I probably had a fracture in my hip and needed an MRI, which they didn't have. The doctor asked if I had any preferences about which hospital I wanted to go to and I replied that since I'd never been to Saint Göran's Hospital before, we would give it a try (I found it funny in the situation that I wanted to try a new hospital that I could give a review of, like on tripadvisor where you rate hotels and restaurants). Once at the hospital, I had an x-ray and was immediately diagnosed with a broken femoral neck. My first reaction was that only old ladies broke their femoral necks and once in the room the tears came. I cried non-stop for days. It was as if the attack was coming back to haunt me. But also the powerlessness with all the shit that was happening to me. It was the first time I'd cried since the rape. So it was necessary.

There are definitely more fun things in the world than operating on a broken femur. I was put back together with a long marrow nail and it was hard. It took a long time for me to get around on my own and the little everyday tasks became big projects. Like moving around, fetching water, showering and going to the toilet. Because I was in so much pain, I was prescribed morphine in tablet form. Taking morphine for so long makes you very unproductive and both Christmas and the New Year were spent in silence. In January I received the expected message from the police. They had been forced to close my case due to a lack of evidence. They'd left no stone unturned but had failed to understand how I'd ended up in hospital and who had attacked me. The police added that they'd found semen in my underwear but unfortunately they hadn't been able to match it to anyone already on the national DNA register. I thought this was crazy and asked myself the rhetorical question: 'who would leave their semen in my underwear without asking permission? But if the man who raped me does the same to someone else, his DNA is now on record and my case can be reopened, which was a small consolation. It became increasingly important for me to get on with my life and not let the experience destroy me and I was determined to make my mark on the public debate.

For me, reporting the crime to the police was a no-brainer. But it's not for everyone.

Unlike many other victims of crime, I was seen and respected by society, which unfortunately isn't a given. It takes a lot to be questioned and mistrusted, while at the same time having to cope and be strong in the practical and emotional process that comes with being a victim of crime.

I learned in a painful way how important it is for society to provide effective legal protection for us citizens. The Consent Act of 2018 was a good start, there were clear changes after that when Parliament decided that a 'no' has meaning and should be respected and not questioned as it was too often before.

I have realised that it is difficult for those closest to me to relate to such a heinous crime as rape and I understand that words are not enough or impossible to find. In my case, I can say that it was easier for many of my loved ones to talk to me about my broken femur, which came a few months later, than about the assault I suffered. As a victim, you need to hear that someone is validating you and caring about you, because how else can you cope?

Any affirmation, big or small, from those closest to you is welcome. I reported the crime to the police, not only for my own sake but also for the sake of others who may not have the strength or courage to do the same in similar situations.

The future

It's a strange situation to summarise one's life in the form of a book. At the same time, writing has been therapeutic for me but it would probably have been easier to write another royal biography than one about myself. However, I think it's very useful to reflect on things when you've been through something as traumatic as being assaulted and raped. In retrospect, I see the event for what it was. It was an attempted murder and it was a miracle that I survived.

Strangely, I feel grateful that I was the victim of the rape and not one of my friends. I know it may sound pretentious but I've always felt that it's easier to fight through difficult situations in your own life than to stand next to someone you care about and feel helpless. I also believe that the many difficult situations I've been through have prepared me for what happened in August 2023. My life hasn't been a bed of roses but the experiences I've had have made me strong. So has my relatively newfound faith.

I decided on early not to dwell on the rape and I've had great aftercare. Not least from my psychiatrist and a physiotherapist. Being able to stop and reflect with them has been very important to my healing. I also learnt breathing techniques and relaxation exercises that helped me to control my thoughts. One of my friends suggested that I try hypnosis to relive every second of the events of that August night. But I'm completely uninterested in that. I have virtually no memory of a twelve-hour period and I'm grateful for that. I have no need to reconstruct the whole course of events but at the same time I fully understand that other victims of crime need to find answers. Nor do I need to identify the perpetrator. The police have done everything they can to find him and also to find out what my own behaviour was on the night in question. Without finding any answers. But because the perpetrator left his semen in my underwear and it's now on the police database, I'm safe in the knowledge that if he ever does it again, the police can arrest him and he'll be punished. Including for what he did to me. I did what I could with my police report. I stood up for myself but also for other potential victims. It feels very important, although I understand that many people don't have the energy to go through all the police interrogations and intimate medical examinations.

Sweden has changed in many ways. Many years of bad policy decisions have left us with one of the most criminal climates in Europe. This is of course unacceptable and I believe that all political representatives have a huge responsibility. Every day we read or see news of bombings, shootings and other atrocities. Often the perpetrators are very young, almost always men and boys. But when do we hear the stories that affect us as victims of crime? We're so much more than a grey mass and a boring statistic. We're people who have had our lives destroyed or severely restricted. We've had our apparent freedom curtailed and everything we do after a violent crime requires careful planning. Can you travel on a particular bus? What time do you have to be at home to feel safe and can you even be in public places?

I think the political debate in Sweden is often ridiculous. Some commentators argue that we shouldn't install surveillance cameras in public places because it violates privacy. I have already pointed out the absurdity of this view. Being raped, as in my case, as a middle-aged man in my own safe neighbourhood, is if anything an invasion of privacy. I find it hard to imagine being filmed and photographed in public as equally horrible. If you have nothing to hide, these tools are a guarantee for a safe society. I feel the same way about the government's newly introduced search zones, which the police have long been calling for. Before I was raped, I hadn't even thought about this need. Now I understand it 100 percent, because no one else should have to go through what I and thousands of other victims of crime go through every year.

According to the Swedish National Council for Crime Prevention (BRÅ), 24, 656 sexual offences were reported in 2022, of which 9635 were classified as rape. Of all residents aged 16-84, 1. 2 per cent of men have reported being the victim of a sexual offence, while the figure for women is 7. 8 per cent. For both men and women, the reporting rate has fallen slightly in recent years and there's a high level of under-reporting, especially among men. Long considered one of the safest countries in the world, Sweden's ruthless crime rate has caused it to fall down all sorts of lists that highlight the safety of European countries. If this can be changed, it will take a long time.

Many of us have become desensitised to the constant shootings, bombings and other serious crimes. It reminds me of the situation in the 1980s when large parts of Africa were hit by a terrible famine. At first, the world was extremely generous and willing to help but after a while, many countries could no longer bear the sight of starving children. The same applies to the invasion of Ukraine: empathy diminishes the longer the war goes on, and I think that's exactly the case with the criminal acts taking place in our country. People can't stand the unimaginable acts because they keep happening. New shootings, new explosions, and often innocent people are affected. It's also important that we as a society stand up and start talking about values. Why are so many young boys fascinated by gang crime and willing to destroy other people? That's a question for which we all have to take responsibility, not just our politicians and authorities but all of us Swedes.

In this book I've tried, to the best of my ability, to put into words what I've suffered through with my mental illness since childhood. Feeling mentally ill is still stigmatised and of course suicide is where the stigma is at its highest. A lot of people think that we shouldn't even talk about it because it might push unhappy people to commit suicide. I think it's quite the opposite. People have always killed themselves because they were unhappy and the only way to make people feel good is to highlight problems and solve them together. Especially when it comes to our young people and their problems.

How are our children really feeling today? A school nurse I spoke to told me that they can tell at an early age if children under ten are unwell. Some children are born with mental health problems, with symptoms such as anxiety, restlessness and difficulty concentrating. Other children may be exposed to various forms of domestic violence and yet remain fiercely loyal to their parents. It sounds incomprehensible but parents are the greatest source of security for all children. I've learnt that there are several things to look out for if children are suffering from mental health problems. A common sign that children may be unwell is when they isolate themselves with video games and show a lack of interest in socialising with other children. It's important for children to play with other children.

Looking at older children, who are teenagers, according to the Swedish National Board of Health, the proportion of 15-year-olds who feel unwell has doubled since the 1980s and one in two young people feels stressed, anxious and generally unwell. There appears to be several reasons for this. These include family structures, the nature of the relationship between children and parents, or whether parents have mental health or substance abuse problems that affect their children. Of course, the socio-economic circumstances of the family also play an important role. Many people, including myself, were financially affected by the corona pandemic. Many of us lost jobs and sources of income. But even before the pandemic, many people had to live on the edge and there was no talk of expensive trips abroad, branded clothes or mobile phones costing thousands of crowns. High interest rates, inflation and our low exchange rate cause anxiety for many of us and this stress is passed on to our children.

School is, of course, another important factor in young people's mental health. As schools are children's workplaces, the school environment is obviously very important. If a pupil is bullied and feels excluded, it becomes difficult and often unbearable. I and many others know exactly what it's like. Many students also feel a lot of pressure to achieve high results, which can lead to various forms of stress.

Not having children myself, I have the deepest respect for anyone who is a parent. I can't think of a more difficult task in life than raising young people and making sure they have the conditions they need to become well-rounded and harmonious adult citizens. Because many children are unhappy, there are certain things you should be aware of as a parent, according to 1177 (a number to call and website for non-emergency care). Children can have many problems: anger and irritability, depression and anxiety, general fatigue and lack of energy, poor appetite, difficulty concentrating, headaches or nausea. I've already touched on sleep problems and the fact that children who feel unwell may shut themselves out from the world around them by burying themselves in video games or other screen-based activities. Everyone needs to get out into the fresh air! There are also children who develop problems with drugs and alcohol at an early age and who express a wish to die. My advice to parents who have children who talk about suicide is to take it very seriously, talk to the child, involve the school health service and the child and adolescent psychiatry service. Unfortunately you have to be strong in these situations. I always say, after all my personal experiences in the health sector, that you have to be healthy to be able to be sick. Because fighting your way through the bureaucracy and getting your rights in a health system that has collapsed in many areas due to severe pressure can be a real pain in the arse.

When you realise that many young people, even in their early teens, are under enormous stress about their future career choices, and that they share so much of their innermost thoughts and feelings with the world on social media, it's easy to feel sad. I think it's just that not everyone is ready to reveal things that are personal. When I was a kid, people had diaries that were locked and hidden from the world after personal feelings were written down. But times are changing, and for many young people today, nothing seems private anymore.

For me, much of my illness has revolved around my sexual orientation. It has often been brought up by people around me but also by strangers, and I've told them about it. Since I came out as gay, I haven't had much need to stand on the barricades with a rainbow flag. It hasn't been my main struggle. I identify first and foremost as a human being but a human being who happens to be gay. However it's unbelievable that my neighbourhood in Södermalm, often described as the most tolerant in the country, could be the scene of a hate crime against a gay man in 2023. Hate and intolerance are everywhere, and if we as a people do not talk about it, we will never solve these serious problems.

Mental health problems are common among LGBTQ youth. According to the Swedish agency for youth and civil society, one in five young people who are LGBTQ say they've been subjected to physical violence by a close relative and many young people have been expelled from their own families. In a major survey conducted by the Swedish National Agency for Youth Affairs in 2010, 25 per cent of gay and bisexual women aged 16-29 who responded said they had tried to kill themselves and among transgender people half had considered suicide. These are frightening statistics and something we must all work to change.

I feel so grateful to be alive. That I've survived my many suicide attempts. According to the Swedish National Board of Health, 1, 254 people died by suicide in Sweden in 2022. Two-thirds of them were men and almost 138 of them were boys under the age of 29. This is roughly how the statistics have looked for many years and in 2018, suicide was the most common cause of death for men aged 15 to 44. Why so many more men than women choose to end their lives is anyone's guess but British professor and suicide researcher Rory O'Connor of the University of Glasgow argues that one of the reasons is that men have a higher physical pain threshold than women. Men are not as afraid of physical pain. Men also don't have the same network of friends that women have, with whom they can easily talk about their problems. There's still a stigma attached to all forms of mental illness and in many situations men feel they have to be 'manly'. Strong. Not vulnerable and caring. It's important for many men to be tough on the outside and I know several men who ended up in wheelchairs after drunkenly throwing themselves out of windows or balconies to end their panic attacks. Perhaps it is unthinkable for them to try therapy, which is really the most natural thing in the world. I think everyone should try therapy at some point in their lives. It can be a strange feeling to leave yourself in the hands of a stranger but every hour of therapy really helps. However, finding the right kind of therap y can be difficult and I think finding the right therapist can be as difficult as finding a partner. You just cannot give up.

Depression, stress and exhaustion are some of the most common reasons why so many people are on sick leave in Sweden today. According to the insurance company Skandia, 48% of sick leave in Sweden is related to mental illness and will cost society 64 billion crowns in 2018. So it's not just a lot of personal tragedy. It's also a national economic disaster and we must all ensure that we make a change to make people feel better. I'm convinced that if this money was spent more on prevention and rehabilitation, many more people would be able to have a regular job and get on with their daily lives. It's important to be able to contribute to our society and to have a professional identity. Staying at home with anxiety and no daily routine only makes things worse. Everyone needs to get out, keep busy and meet other people. I shudder to think what these figures and statistics will look like in a few years' time, with the enormous damage the pandemic has done to us people. It will probably take many, many years to recover from the psychological damage caused to many of us by covid-19, the war in Ukraine and the economy. We all long for a better future and less hateful rhetoric from our leaders around the world.

For many years I identified with my mental illness. I felt safe in feeling bad. But thanks to my faith, amazing friends and great community support, I dared to feel good and stop living in bitterness. It's important to have the courage to ask for help, and although it often feels impossible, help is out there. Sometimes it can be the person you least expect standing by your side.

For me, it's now even more important to work with vulnerable children around the world but also to share my life experiences. No matter how long I live, I feel that I want to be able to contribute to a better world and especially to give young people the message that it is possible to turn the darkest into a positive future. Because if I could do it, anyone can.

Quick guide to how I took control and turned my life from chaos to balance

- *The importance of making choices. When you choose, you create direction, which turned out to be one of the most powerful tools in my life.*
- *Change is a natural part of life. So be prepared for life to change quickly, both positively and negatively.*
- *Get rid of energy thieves, not only people but also your own behaviours and poor life choices.*
- *Recognise your high value!*
- *Actively connect with your spiritual side, we're not just a physical mass but much more.*
- *Notice the jewels in everyday life, such as your favourite ice cream or a parking space that presents itself to you. This is how you live each day.*

- *It's ok to have a breakdown sometimes, to be confused, to have no answers, to be angry and disappointed. It takes the pressure off. Because, you know, nobody really knows what we're doing here. Everyone is confused sometimes.*

- *Even if you feel bad, it's good for your wellbeing to get involved with others who need help. This doesn't mean that you should neglect your own needs. You can do both, try it, you will feel better.*

- *Dare to acknowledge and talk about uncomfortable things, be it illness, insults, grief, the list goes on.*

- *Dare to try, it's perfectly alright to 'fail'. I can guarantee that all successful entrepreneurs have gone through a number of 'failures' before they get it right.*